Praise for *Each Day a New Beginning* Workbook

"What Karen found in Alcoholics Anonymous, and what I found in the course, was a path to God that wasn't waylaid by religious dogma."

—Marianne Williamson, *New York Times* bestselling author of *A Return to Love*

"Casey's voice is thoughtful and accessible. Readers with a belief in the power of God will be most amenable to her recommendations for a simpler, more rewarding life."

—*Publishers Weekly*

"Karen Casey is a wise woman who has written more than twenty books based on her own experiences, including her long-time spiritual practices with the Twelve Steps and *A Course in Miracles*. Her writing and her speaking have affected millions of lives."

—Jan Johnson, publisher emerita, Conari Press

"Karen Casey teaches us how to row our boat (note: not other people's boats) gently down the stream. When we row gently, we don't yell about who or what must be on the bank around the bend. We peacefully accept what comes, and this makes us very merry."

—Hugh Prather, author of *Morning Notes* and *The Little Book of Letting Go*

"You just can't go wrong with Karen Casey."

—Earnie Larsen, author of *Stage II Recovery: Life Beyond Addiction* and *From Anger to Forgiveness*

"With wisdom and encouragement forged in the kiln of personal experience, author Karen Casey's *Each Day a New Beginning* offers a daily path to self-compassion, confidence, and contentment that is invaluable to any woman, but especially those whose lives have been touched by addiction."

—Sue Patton Thoele, author of *The Courage to Be Yourself*, *The Woman's Book of Strength*, and *How to Stay Upbeat in a Beat Down World*

"The value of the workbook for *Each Day a New Beginning* is priceless. This is a great opportunity to deepen one's understanding not only of themselves but of the world opening up around them. This workbook will definitely help the reader to look deeper into their recovery and help them to examine their path as they take this workbook and their recovery one day at a time, one reading at a time."

—Joan R., Minneapolis, fifty years sober

"In another remarkable contribution to recovery literature, Karen Casey offers a highly-effective tool: writing. Her *Each Day a New Beginning Workbook*, a fabulous companion to her bestselling daily reader, provides effective support and guidance. Perfect for individual or group use, this useful workbook is destined to become a staple in the lives of those who aim to rise above the tide of addiction."

—Nita Sweeney, bestselling author of *Depression Hates a Moving Target* and *Make Every Move a Meditation*

"Need a fresh start? Read this book—every day! Karen Casey gifts us with the sense of starting anew with each turn of the calendar page. When we open up to the daily quote, tiny teaching, and easy-to-remember mantra, we offer ourselves a fresh outlook and new possibility. What I love the best is that these daily teachings come in bite-sized nuggets—small enough to digest fairly easily, but still with enough thought-provoking goodness to chew on! Casey gives us exactly what we need each day to connect to the people around us, to our spirits, and to new ways of being alive. She helps us navigate the hard stuff, too. *Each Day a New Beginning Workbook* is filled with gems of wisdom! If you need more peace in your life, this book is for you!"

—Sherry Richert Belul, founder of Simply Celebrate and author of *Say It Now: 33 Creative Ways to Say I Love You to the Most Important People in Your Life*

"Karen Casey's *Each Day a New Beginning* is a classic and timeless book for the woman in recovery from alcoholism. The daily entries provide a helpful resource to one's spiritual toolkit. I thoroughly recommend it to the newcomer in recovery, as well as those with many years of sobriety. This *Each Day a New Beginning Workbook* will be a daily companion for me and many others in their recovery. Thank you for your love and service, Karen Casey."

—Kim, twelve years sober

Each
Day a
New
Beginning
Workbook

Books by Karen Casey

Each Day a New Beginning
Each Day a Renewed Beginning
Let Go Now: Embracing Detachment
Codependence and the Power of Detachment
It's Up to You
Change Your Mind and Your Life Will Follow
20 Things I Know for Sure
Getting Unstuck
The Good Stuff from Growing Up in a Dysfunctional Family
Living Long, Living Passionately
All We Have Is All We Need
Be Who You Want to Be
Peace a Day at a Time
52 Ways to Live the Course in Miracles
In God's Care
A Woman's Spirit
Daily Meditations for Practicing the Course
Worthy of Love
A Life of My Own
The Promise of a New Day
Keepers of the Wisdom
Fearless Relationships
My Story to Yours
Serenity
If Only I Could Quit
Girl to Girl

Each Day a New Beginning Workbook

Daily Meditations for Women Faced with Adversity

Karen Casey

mango
PUBLISHING GROUP
CORAL GABLES

For permission requests, please contact the publisher at:
Mango Publishing Group
2850 S Douglas Road, 2nd Floor
Coral Gables, FL 33134 USA
info@mango.bz

For special orders, quantity sales, course adoptions and corporate sales, please email the publisher at sales@mango.bz. For trade and wholesale sales, please contact Ingram Publisher Services at customer.service@ingramcontent.com or +1.800.509.4887.

Each Day a New Beginning Workbook: Daily Meditations for Women Faced with Adversity

Library of Congress Cataloging-in-Publication number: has been requested
ISBN: (pb) 978-1-68481-488-6, (e) 978-1-68481-489-3
BISAC category code: SEL006000, SELF-HELP / Substance Abuse & Addictions / Alcohol

Dedication

I want to dedicate this book to all the women and men who have sought guidance from my first book, *Each Day a New Beginning*, or any of my other books over the last forty-two years. The connections we have made over the decades astound me every single day. Without your presence, my life would have felt very empty, very hollow. I know without a doubt that our meeting once again here has been by divine appointment. And I thank you for journeying with me all of these years.

May our journey continue and may you know peace, a day at a time.

Blessings always,
Karen

"It's your reaction to adversity, not adversity itself, that determines how your life's story will develop."

—Dieter F. Uchtdorf

Contents

Preface

Hi friends,

I'm paying a visit once again. Many of you met me for the first time forty years ago when *Each Day a New Beginning: Daily Meditations for Women* was first published. And in the forty years that have passed since then, many more of you have come along for the journey, one that has hopefully inspired you in many ways.

Quite possibly you met me in another one of the books I have written over the forty-eight years of my own recovery in Alcoholics Anonymous. Perhaps we even crossed paths at a workshop or talk I gave. The real point is, it matters not where or when we met. We are connecting now, and that pleases me.

This workbook has your own journey in mind. No matter whether you have been on this recovery path for a long time or if you are just exploring whether you want to even be on it, I think the ideas and questions to ponder and write about will appeal to you. I personally think we can never know too much about ourselves. Our roots, along with our many stopping off points along the way to where we find ourselves today, are rich with the information I believe we need to make the most of the years we have left. Heaven knows, at eighty-four, I do think I still have more growing to do. I'm pretty sure you do too. And that's the good news. We are never done until that moment when we are called to embrace the final leg of our journey.

It's my hope that you will love every moment you spend delving into this workbook and that you will be surprised again and again by all that you are inspired to explore, perhaps for the first time or for the hundredth time; both learning and then embracing all that your memory has gifted you with.

Most of all, have fun. There is no time like the present to find out who we are and where we may yet need to go.

Love to you as we move forward together.

Karen

Introduction

Why a workbook? Here are some ideas that I think are worth pondering:

- Engaging with a workbook from day to day pushes us to delve deep within ourselves, which becomes ever more necessary if we want to grow in our recovery.

- The willingness to consider the fond memories of our past, along with the struggles that pushed us forward, allows us to know who we are and may well point us in a new direction too.

- A workbook is designed to explore the interior of our hearts and minds. The better we know ourselves, the greater will be our chance for long-term recovery, if that's what we desire, as well as peaceful living.

- Because a workbook is done incrementally, we are not overwhelmed with the prospect of looking at the totality of who we are now—or of who we were back then.

- Why is it important to look at who we were? We can't really appreciate who we are now without a detailed overview of how we got here.

- The big question for most of us to ask is where do I want to go? The groundwork you are laying in this workbook will be crucial as you move forward in life.

- You will see that there hasn't been a single experience that was superfluous. In fact, each one opened the door to what needed to come next.

- The good news is a workbook such as this has the capacity to change your trajectory from here forward.

- No thought you are inspired to reflect on will be wasted. Each one of them is its own "aha" moment.

- The evidence of God's presence on your journey is everywhere. Noting those memories as they surface can be mind-altering.

- The primary gift of a workbook is what you will learn from your reflections.

- Charting a new life course might be where the workbook leads you. Or it might direct you instead to revisit certain times and places that you never fully embraced. Either way, you are being guided—always.

These ideas will be fleshed out as you move forward. Have fun as you advance through these pages and grow. Who knows where this may lead you? But God knows. And that's a promise.

How to Use This Workbook

The good news is that you get to decide how you want to use this workbook. There are no musts. If you want to explore the table of contents and then turn to the chapter that calls to you right away, please do so. There is no perfect order to this exploration. It's your journey, after all, through your life. You can decide to spend a few minutes every morning, after reading a meditation book perhaps; or mid-afternoon when you need time away from what has engaged you all day.

Personally, I have always liked to take some time closer to the end of the day to clear my mind and then allow it to open to an idea that's calling to me. And I do think you will find many ideas calling to you in this workbook.

Let me reiterate, you can begin on any chapter you choose and then back up to an earlier one. No one is in charge but you. The point is, enjoy the process. Enjoy your discoveries. In particular, enjoy where you note you have been and where you seem to be interested in exploring next. This is your only life, after all. Celebrate it one thought at a time, one journal entry at a time.

Chapter 1

....

Daily Practices

Daily practices may include prayer and meditation, exercise of a particular kind, yoga, or writing a note to God; whatever we choose to make a part of our daily round, they all ground us for the day ahead. Each one of us will always experience a better start on the day if we have gotten grounded first.

The fortunate thing is that there is no one way to ground ourselves. And we need not do it in the same way every day. One day we may be entirely focused on prayer and meditation. Another day our time may be better spent sitting quietly in a yoga class. I personally find that sitting a spell and connecting with God through the written word or a simple conversation prepares me for a day of greater peace; and peace is what I hunger for most, these days.

The point is that you need to follow your own heart. In fact, that's the strong suggestion I'd make to each of you throughout your travels in this workbook. Your heart will never lead you astray. It's always under the direction of the God of your understanding.

A Beginning

Although each day is a new beginning, pondering a few of the days that have gone before can help the next to gift us with even more meaning. But what does that mean? Let's stop for a moment and consider this in greater depth. Whatever is on its way to you today—and something is on its way—is part of the plan for your life. Does that make sense to you? Just stop and consider for a moment a few of the events that happened just in the last few days. Do you see how one event was actually tied to what happened previously? Hmmm. No accidents here. *Let's jot a few thoughts down about what this idea calls to mind. This is a great way to launch our daily practice.*

Let's write:

_____

_____

_____

_____

_____

_____

_____

_____

_____

_____

_____

_____

_____

_____

_____

_____

_____

_____

_____

Did you take note of how perfectly the events unfolded? Even if we didn't like all of them, they moved us forward. You can put that idea in the bank.

Indeed, life is like a bridge hand. One card played leads to the next right choice. And it dictates what perhaps should come next as well. Now, a hand can be played poorly, for sure. But then the next hand is dealt and another chance to play smarter presents itself. *Life is like a card game in this way. And we get to see how the cards fall, one card at a time.*

Moving On

We all reflect, and we should make that part of our daily practice. Some consider it daydreaming, but I think it's valuable mind work. We can't know who we are or what value any experience has brought to our lives if we don't spend some time in reflection. I'm certain that's true for you, or else this workbook wouldn't have appealed to you. What is it that keeps drawing your attention these days? We all know how a pulled tooth keeps calling to our tongue to fill in the gap. What's drawing your attention into some gap in your mind at the present time? And it doesn't have to be a big deal experience either. Even those tiny ones that seemed so unimportant at the time might not be done with us. How exciting is that? *It's time to reflect on at least one of them now. Reflections inform us in ways that add to our wholeness.*

Let's write:

_____

_____

_____

_____

_____

_____

_____

_____

_____

_____

_____

_____

_____

_____

_____

_____

_____

_____

_____

_____

_____

_____

Are you beginning to connect some dots? That's really the value of reflecting. You didn't get to where you are right now by accident, even though your journey sometimes appeared haphazard. Nothing about these life passages were ever haphazard. *There was intention in everything. And guess what? God was part of everything too.*

Another Step Forward

As Dorothy Bryant said in the quote on January 3 of *Each Day a New Beginning*: "Like an old gold-panning prospector, you must resign yourself to digging up a lot of sand from which you will later patiently wash out a few particles of gold ore." Every day, as part of our daily practice, it makes sense to see what gold appeared as recently as yesterday. For sure there was some. We may have to ponder for a few moments because of our tendency to dismiss things as unimportant. Nothing is unimportant. Nothing!

Can you make a list of some of your "particles of gold" in this past week or longer? For sure they were there. Can you see how you have been affected?

Let's write the list:

_____

_____

_____

_____

_____

_____

_____

_____

As I mentioned earlier, nothing has gone for naught—nothing! We have needed and will always need every experience, big or tiny, that pays a visit. That's how we become who we are, and no one else is like us. No one anywhere will ever be quite like us—not ever. Pretty cool, huh?

Do you have some thoughts about this that you'd like to share?

_____

_____

_____

_____

_____

_____

_____

_____

_____

_____

_____

If Only

Everyone wishes for a do-over, at least occasionally. No doubt this is true for you too. Perhaps we don't think of this idea as falling into the category of daily practice, but I think it comfortably does. By revisiting how we showed up as recently as yesterday, we just may discover an example of a "do-over" opportunity. Making a habit of a quick review (which can be a bit like doing a tenth step at a moment's notice) can certainly help us to change who we are by taking the opportunity to address who we were in a moment that wasn't our best. And doing this can give us examples of situations that might be helped in our daily prayer and meditation.

I've certainly had my occasions for do-over wishes over the many decades of my life. Some were serious infractions. But the majority were much less significant. However, they all need to be accounted for, admitted to, and addressed in a loving way in the hopes that our disrespect can be forgiven. The fallout that arises from not addressing these situations lingers and then interferes with whatever hopes we had for a peaceful day ahead.

Take a few moments and quietly consider what calls to you as a "do-over" opportunity. It could be a recent experience or one in the distant past. If it's still hanging around in your memory, it needs to be addressed. Then write about this experience as it was when it took place and why you think doing something different now would bring you greater joy and peace of mind. How might the other party or parties be impacted in a different way? In fact, can you address the other party or parties and make things right now?

Let's write:

_____

_____

_____

_____

_____

_____

_____

_____

_____

_____

_____

_____

_____

_____

The real joy in this is that we can quite possibly better anticipate more thoughtful options for our lives as we move forward, and as we change our thinking, making better choices will prevent us from needing to wish for too many do-overs down the line.

What Moves Your Life Forward?

According to Marie Curie, "I was taught that the way of progress is neither swift nor easy." Her assessment should free us from pushing ourselves too hard. Progress is incremental, no matter what our chosen field of work or study. And the good news is that we really do have all the time we need to inch forward. Usually we are the only ones who are measuring our progress and deeming it adequate or not. And if we are in a situation where someone else is watching over our shoulder all of the time, perhaps it's time for a change in what we want to do with our lives.

Indeed, life is to be enjoyed, and if you can't find joy in what you have chosen to do and progress seems beyond your reach, it just may be that God is calling you to consider a new direction, perhaps a new option for your chosen line of work. How does this idea strike you today? Are you really doing what you want to do? Are you feeling like you are progressing in the direction you want to go?

These questions are great ones to ponder with the help of prayer and meditation. They may be explored as well by journaling about them. Sitting and having that all-important conversation with God might steer you in the right direction too. The point is, you and I have so many ways we can seek the guidance we need.

Let's reflect on these questions for a time. Are you doing what you really want to do? If not, open your heart to share where you are today and where you may prefer to be going.

Let's write:

_____

_____

If you are completely content, what has helped you be that way?

_____

_____

_____

_____

_____

_____

_____

_____

_____

_____

_____

_____

_____

_____

_____

The Promise of Daily Practice

Recovery is a whole new ballgame, isn't it? Everything about it is impacted by our daily practices. What most surprises you about how your life has changed and how these practices have helped you turn the corner?

_____

_____

_____

_____

_____

_____

_____

_____

If you are like me, you had no idea when you walked into this new life what it was really going to mean. I had not a clue when I went to that first meeting that the desire to drink would be lifted from me starting that night until this very day, more than forty-eight years later. Without a doubt, God did for me what I could not have done for myself.

As I sit here today, I am quite convinced that God is still very present and "on call" to my every need. And I wholeheartedly believe that He always was and will always remain so. What evidence do you see that this has been true for you as well?

Let's write:

_____

_____

_____

_____

_____

_____

_____

_____

_____

_____

_____

Isn't it simply amazing to spend a few moments recalling a handful of the tiny ways God showed up on our journey? And isn't it even more interesting to take note of those times we can now see that He was there, totally unbeknownst to us? *Remember, He was always there—and can never be elsewhere!*

Chapter 2

....

Dreams Can Be
Our Guideposts

Dreams really are not superfluous to our journeys; they are essential to our existence. Whether they are sleeping dreams or those we have during quiet meditation, journaling, or our morning walk, I think what our inner guide is trying to convey to us is deeply embedded in our dreams. And that's an idea that should excite us. We are never just wandering alone on this path that has called to us. We are always being led in one direction or another. And that's pretty exciting, I'd say.

Great scientists like Albert Einstein, Thomas Edison, Marie Curie, and Dorothy Hodgkin had great dreams too, and our lives are the better for them. One can never be certain just how much impact any one of our dreams might have on someone else today or at some point in the future. Let's just never discount them as irrelevant, particularly to us or to those whose paths we will cross in our lifetime.

Dreams May Well Be Our Guiding Stars

According to Eleanor Roosevelt, "The future belongs to those who believe in the beauty of their dreams." I find that an interesting quote. I do think dreams, and not necessarily those we have while sleeping, can direct our steps in a new direction. A dream can simply be a longing for a change of some kind in our lives. And it doesn't even need to be one that's thought out in any detailed fashion.

For instance, I love to write. I loved it even as a young girl. But then when I was in graduate school, I realized a whole new level of love, embedded in a deep comfort to my soul, that came every time I sat with legal pad and pen and wrote the many papers that were required of all doctoral students. I never dreaded any one of them. In fact, they always gave me solace. I could sense with each one that the words seemed to be flowing out of the end of my pen. The same was true for my three-hundred-page dissertation too. I didn't know at the time that my future was calling to me, but hindsight has revealed that.

When I finished my degree, I knew I wanted to be a writer. I didn't know just how that was going to manifest, but God knew. I dutifully "showed up."

I think this may be how dreams work for most of us. We feel a calling to move in one direction or another. And if we are willing to listen, the rest is history.

Do you sense that you have been called to do something in particular in your life? Explore what that has been.

Let's write:

_____

_____

_____

_____

_____

_____

_____

_____

_____

_____

_____

_____

_____

_____

_____

_____

A Familiar Refrain

I'd like to suggest that you select a meditation that has always called to you from *Each Day a New Beginning*, perhaps one that you read on a special day in your life or one that comforted you when you were going through a really tough time. Quote a few lines from that meditation, and then delve into it, sharing why it grabbed your attention: why it has been remembered by you, and what about it gave you comfort then and perhaps even today, a few months or even years later.

Be as open and honest as you can when you revisit this suggestion for writing:

_____

_____

_____

_____

_____

_____

_____

_____

_____

Dare to Dream

Is your imagination calling to you today?

"My imagination will serve me today. It will offer me ideas and the courage to go forth." This quote from *Each Day a New Beginning* is calling to us every day if we allow it to. We have to dare to be courageous and let our imaginations, our dreams, roam free. But are we giving free rein to our imagination? Each one of us must answer that for ourselves.

How might you answer that question today? What evidence substantiates your answer? Ponder a while, perhaps, before writing:

_____

_____

_____

_____

_____

_____

_____

_____

Another Moment Calls to Us

We are never standing still. Even if we haven't left our couch or our chair, or even our bed, our minds have not been still. They are seldom still all by themselves. We can quiet them, of course, and do on occasion. But our minds usually churn and push and even conjure up worries if left to themselves. Then, if we are vigilant, we remember to focus on these words: *God grant me the serenity to accept the things I cannot change; the courage to change the things I can. And the wisdom to know the difference.* We ask God to calm our minds and quiet our hearts, and then we can move forward peacefully.

What does it mean to you to move forward peacefully? When did you last do this with good results?

Let's share here:

_____

_____

_____

_____

_____

_____

_____

Let's Pause for a While

Revisiting our lives as we are doing in this workbook can be considered both helpful and a bit daunting. Sometimes we don't want to recall past events, particularly if they were painful when first experienced. But even those recollections can offer us new insights, and that's what we are seeking here, new insights about old experiences. Let's never forget that nary a single one of them happened by chance. *We are always in the right place at the right time for what is perfect for the next leg of our journey.* And for sure, let's remember that God, as we understand God, was always present. Why don't we invite God to revisit these experiences with us? Perhaps that will help us to seek the hidden gifts each one actually bestowed on us.

Are you ready to invite God in for a second look? What can you see with His help that you might have missed initially? Dig deep. There is no hurry.

Ready to write?

_____

_____

_____

_____

_____

_____

_____

Turning to *Each Day* for a Moment

As I said in *Each Day a New Beginning*, *"Resistance to the events, the situations, the many people who come into our lives, blocks the growth we are offered every day."* Nothing that comes to us is superfluous. Nothing. That's a strong statement, isn't it? It means the lost job, or the relationship that ended, or even the fire that took away the house that was our home had a message for us.

Perhaps these particular examples don't fit the timeline of your life, but there were experiences you lived through that you didn't love. That's the nature of being alive.

It's time to take a look and see what the reward hidden in the rubble was. There was one. And there always will be one. Rest your mind a moment, then recall a few examples of the rubble and what was gleaned in the aftermath. Give your mind plenty of time to discover what needs to be shared.

Now, let's write:

_____

_____

_____

_____

_____

_____

Books Can Lead Us to Insight

As guideposts, books too can move us to new understandings. They may well ignite a totally new dream or a new awareness, leading to a new direction.

I well remember when I read John Powell's book *Why Am I Afraid to Tell You Who I Am?* There was one simple comment uttered by his friend Sidney Harris, a journalist, that got my attention like no other. In response to a question posed by Powell after they had purchased a newspaper from a New York vendor, Harris said something that turned my world upside down. The vendor had been exceedingly rude. Yet Harris was kind in return and even tipped him. Powell was dumbstruck and asked, why were you so nice? Harris replied, "Why should I let him decide what kind of day I am going to have?" My entire life up to that point was a series of responses that were always related to how others had treated me—always. And I truly didn't know that I had another choice until that moment.

Take a few moments to think about a book that you read, either recently or a long time ago—I read the one I describe above in 1971—that moved you to change in a way you hadn't previously considered. Perhaps it was a self-help book, or maybe a biography of someone you admired, or a history book about an era or certain events you had failed to appreciate when studying about them in school. What's important is that you were changed by the book's contents. Before beginning to write, refresh your memories and recall who you were before reading the book. How did it help you to change? Who are you now?

What fun it is to revisit our lives in this way. What was the book? What is coming first to your mind? In what way have you specifically changed? Why is it still lingering in your mind? Enjoy this exercise. Hopefully it will ignite a great awareness in you.

Let's write:

_____

_____

_____

_____

_____

_____

_____

_____

_____

_____

_____

_____

_____

_____

Before leaving this idea, is there another book that runs a close second to this one you have already written about? What about it is calling to you at this moment?

Please share:

_____

_____

_____

_____

_____

_____

_____

_____

_____

_____

_____

Vulnerability Invites Vulnerability

Let's consider vulnerability and how, like our dreams, it may also help us to move in a new direction. It might also serve to help someone else who is watching. The real point is that our dreams manifest in many ways. And those moments of vulnerability can produce even more dreams. Let's always be on the lookout as we consider our experiences of being vulnerable:

In *Each Day a New Beginning*, I wrote: "*Vulnerability is as much a part of being human as is strength… Our soft edges invite others' openness and their expressions of love.*" Not only their expressions of love are invited, but perhaps also their willingness to share those dreams that are prompting them to take heart and move in a new direction. When any one of us feels safe in the company of someone else, we are far more comfortable allowing our inner selves to be known. And the more any one of us can share that part of our being, the greater will be the movement forward for all of us.

I feel quite certain that we all want to be recipients of love and acceptance, along with also hoping for a cheering section too for our bravery in making a dream into a reality. But when any one of us is brittle and hard to be around, expressions of love from others might come sparingly. What has been your experience with vulnerability? Do others share with you openly? Do you feel safe in sharing too?

It's time for pondering. It might well be time for soul-searching and a change in habits as well. Let's rest a few minutes with these ideas and these questions before beginning to write:

_____

_____

_____

_____

_____

_____

_____

_____

_____

_____

_____

_____

_____

_____

_____

_____

_____

The Joy of an "Aha" Moment

Hopefully you have had at least one or two of these moments since beginning to review your life in these pages. They are the moments that gift us with enlightenment. They quite often surprise us, too; in ways we'd never have expected. They can well be embedded in a "dream," particularly one that drifts before our eyes while meditating or even while strolling on our favorite path.

One of my "aha" moments was becoming aware that if my first husband had not chosen to leave me for another woman, I would never have attempted getting a PhD. I had not been a stellar student as an undergraduate. I was a party girl, and studying took a back seat to that. Graduate school was certainly not on my radar screen. I'm convinced it was on God's "screen," however. And that experience sent me in an entirely new direction in life.

You are in fact holding in your hands, right now, a product of that new direction. Although it took God and me some time to get from there to here, we made it. And how grateful I am. There were a host of other books before this one came along, but every one of them, I now realize, was part of that initial "aha" awareness. Isn't life simply grand?

You have had these moments of realization too. I know you have. Take some time now to corner them in your memory. You will love discovering them.

What have you discovered? Wallow in the joy of the discovery. Then write about it:

_____

_____

_____

Chapter 3

·····························

Inner Peace Is
Our Birthright

Although inner peace may be our birthright, far too few of us live in
that space on a consistent basis. There are of course many reasons for
that. One that comes quickly to mind is that we are too often consumed
with what someone else is doing. As a friend of mine in Al-Anon said in a
meeting many years ago: "There's two kinds of business; my business and
none of my business." And when I am paying too much attention, to you
and your business, I will never experience the inner peace that could be
available to me.

How nice that peace can be claimed at a moment's notice. All I have to do
is seek it, and nothing else. Of course, this means allowing the others on
my path to make whatever journey they are here to make. Even though we
have encountered one another, that does not mean we have been assigned
the job of being in charge of the trajectory of each other's journeys to their
destination. While observing one another may teach us something we need to
know, exerting control—or trying to—will never bless our journey or theirs.

Inner peace: Just the mere mention of it is calming. Wouldn't you agree?
And I know, particularly since aging, that I want a quiet life, one that's not
in constant turmoil because of what others are doing. And when I say others,
I mean strangers as well as friends and family members. Being at peace is a
choice we each have the option to make for ourselves, regardless of what or
who might be vying for our attention.

The added plus, from my perspective, is that when we greet others peacefully, we might have a positive impact on their choices too. I'm thinking it's worth the effort.

Let's look at some options for ourselves and how we can move forward more peacefully.

Take a Turn to a Better Direction

Some days, peace may be the farthest thing from our minds and all we really want to do is pull the covers over our head. On those days we really don't care about peace, our own or anyone else's. You know you have the right to choose to retreat or strategically withdraw. Hiding under the covers may be in order. And perhaps you need to take advantage of that option. However, there's something else we might try instead, and that is turning our thoughts to someone else. Might someone need help at this moment? I don't mean to imply we should ever codependently turn our attention away from ourselves in order to control someone else, but wallowing in self-pity will never give us the inner peace we desire and deserve. In fact, it can often best be alleviated by listening to someone else who needs a listening ear. We both may feel better for it, and we might even feel the gift of peace. Just maybe…

What has been your most recent experience with helping someone else that ultimately helped you too?

Share a story:

_____

_____

_____

_____

_____

_____

_____

_____

_____

_____

You know, the good thing about helping someone else is that they may well be inspired to help another person too. One good turn leads to another—always. And you can be the one who initiates this positive feedback loop among your circle of friends.

How does this make you feel? A short reflection perhaps:

_____

_____

_____

_____

_____

_____

_____

_____

How's It Going?

If you've been moving through the chapters of this workbook in sequence, it just might be time to review what kind of help you have received so far from addressing these myriad suggestions for reflection in the first few chapters. Your commitment to follow each of them with a bit of writing might have been a bit of a stretch, but in a good way, I hope. The big question is this: Have these ideas and suggestions for writing honestly been helpful? It's surely my hope the answer is yes, but only you know for sure.

Perhaps listing a few of the ways you have been helped, or hopefully moved to revisit your past, is worth a few additional comments. Who knows? You very likely will want to review this workbook and its contents at a future date. I know I get greater awareness about who I have become when I look more closely at who I was.

It's time to write. How have you been helped so far? Your list need not be long, but flesh it out if you want to learn more about yourself:

_____

_____

_____

_____

_____

_____

Swimming Toward Serenity

Changing a behavior can be a turning point and if we want greater peace, this may be crucial. No doubt we all have a few behaviors that need changing, or at least refining because of how they impact others, as well as ourselves. The following quote from my book *Each Day a New Beginning* might change your trajectory:

> *"The change of one simple behavior can affect other behaviors and thus change many things."*
>
> —Jean Baer

I know that with the help of Al-Anon, I have changed a lot of my behaviors, particularly those that negatively impact my most significant relationships. For instance, not letting the mood swings of others determine my actions was huge for me. Of course, I still get caught off guard on occasion, and react rather than pausing to let the moment pass. But progress has been made. And it's the little successes that add up to bringing me closer to being the person I really want to be, a person who lives with greater peace of mind.

I've found it truly refreshing and enlightening to find that a tiny change I can make can change so much about the course of my life. I used to think I needed to find clever ways to get others to change if I wanted the everyday affairs of my life to change. How wrong I was. My peace, and yours too, is a choice, plain and simple. And we can have it moment by moment, even all day if that's what we have decided to focus on and if we have committed to change the only behaviors we can ever hope to change: our own.

How about you? What have you learned about changing a behavior or two that too often turned your world upside down? A world upside down will never be a peaceful world; this I know for sure.

Share a memory, perhaps an old one, or else one that happened just yesterday. It matters not. That a change in your behavior transpired is what counts. Please also comment on whether that change resulted in greater peace of mind. After all, that's what we are seeking.

Let's write:

_____

_____

_____

_____

_____

_____

_____

_____

_____

_____

_____

_____

What Will This Day Offer You?

Each day is a new beginning, and each day, along with being new, offers us a host of never before anticipated opportunities to enjoy greater peace. How lucky we are indeed.

It's quite possible that many of us have never even looked at life this way before. I certainly remember periods of my life when the new opportunities facing me made me far more uneasy than I do when seeing them as avenues to peace of mind.

Yesterday is gone. And tomorrow will come when it should. *But today is here, to be grasped with both hands and an open mind and heart.* Let's look at these ideas in greater detail today. What about yesterday was possibly a great lesson or experience?

Share a thought here:

_____

_____

_____

_____

_____

_____

_____

_____

Has it dawned on you that there may be something you are seeing or feeling right now, today, that you want to wholeheartedly grab on to?

Share what that might be:

_____

_____

_____

_____

_____

_____

_____

_____

_____

_____

_____

_____

What have you learned from your travels through this assignment about all of our tomorrows that speaks to you right now?

Share those ideas here:

_____

_____

_____

_____

_____

_____

_____

_____

_____

_____

_____

_____

Is there a book that you read in the past, one that inspired greater moments of inner peace, that may still be worthy of continued reflection? Perhaps that book broadened your capacity for enjoying peace in a more sustained way in your daily travels.

Share some thoughts here for your chance to review again what you learned from it that has mattered to you over the years. Giving peace a chance isn't just a glib saying, is it? Some thoughts please:

_____

_____

_____

_____

_____

_____

_____

_____

_____

_____

_____

_____

Life Moves Forward, Hopefully One Peaceful Moment at a Time

No person you ever met was insignificant to your journey through life. Every moment ushered someone into your presence that you needed to encounter. And that's the real joy we can count on for the rest of our lives.

Who comes quickly to mind right now? Do you care to speculate on why they popped up? And can you see how you exchanged lessons learned with that person or people?

Ponder for a bit and then write about those lessons:

_____

_____

_____

_____

_____

_____

_____

_____

_____

Return to Contentment

Standing still isn't really an option, is it, if someone is trying to disrupt our peace of mind?

Time moves on, moment by moment. Our willingness to experience each moment as it comes, remembering that it's always in the company of the God of our understanding, is where contentment and peace of mind greet us. To be the recipient of constant contentment is truly a heavenly gift. And it is ours for the taking!

Are there moments you can recall from the last few days where you felt deep inner peace? What inspired these feelings?

Revisiting those moments can encourage more of them.

It's time to share a moment or two of that contentment:

_____

_____

_____

_____

_____

_____

_____

A Blessing That Came Calling

Probably everyone sitting with this workbook today is able, with hindsight, to appreciate an experience that turned out to be a blessing even though it might not have felt like one when it initially came calling. That is certainly true for me. Here's my story:

When I first got sober, I struggled to feel the presence of God. While at meetings, He felt relatively close, but then when I went home, the feeling was gone. Because writing gave me peace of mind, I began writing "to God," more or less. I could feel His presence while I sat in the beat-up old brown recliner that my father-in-law had given me. I still didn't feel Him consistently, but moments of feeling Him were much appreciated.

Those journal pages ultimately became my first book: *Each Day a New Beginning*. That had certainly not been on my radar screen, but I knew it was on God's—in time. We simply don't always know the real importance of an event while it's happening.

Isn't that exciting?

Please share something that comes to your mind now that was steering you in a new direction, unbeknownst to you. Perhaps you can see how it was a peaceful turning point for you like mine was for me.

Let's write:

_____

_____

_____

Inviting Guidance, Cultivating Patience

Clarity will always come if we are patient. Peace of mind often accompanies the clarity. Something I wrote in *Each Day a New Beginning* more than forty years ago still rings so true: "Our wants in life may be simple, or they may be complex. They may yet be confused in our minds, but the clarity will come if we are patient."

Patience is the necessary ingredient. And it's not always easy to be patient. In fact, it's seldom easy to be patient. But remembering that we will always know what we need to know when the time is right can be helpful, and it will invariably offer us a refresher course in peace of mind too. God is in charge, has always been, and will always remain so. If you are struggling with patience or a lack of peace of mind—and most of us are, more often than we like to admit—the "Serenity Prayer" is one avenue to discovering both.

Are you seeking clarity and direction about some situation today? How might the "Serenity Prayer" help you?

It's a good time to share what's heavy on our minds:

_____

_____

_____

_____

_____

Taking Another Look at Life's Patterns

"It is no accident that I am here."

The above quote from my book *Each Day a New Beginning* comforts me even more as I age. *There simply are no accidents!* And what peace of mind this gives me. I think in my youth and even in early recovery, I was quite often confounded by where I was and nothing seemed "just right." Not only was I confounded in my childhood, I was anxious about what lay ahead in every instance. My stormy household didn't offer the security I sought. There was no physical abuse present, but anger leading to emotional upset was the constant. The household simply wasn't peaceful. I didn't even know what feeling at peace meant in those days.

And then in my first marriage, I was dumped for another woman. I was devastated and embarrassed. What would others think of me? I certainly didn't see that as the first door opening to an incredibly beautiful life, one that is continuing to unfold in this, my eighty-fourth year. I would never have known what peace meant if a few doors hadn't closed in my earlier years.

So how can I claim that there "is no accident" regarding wherever I or we are? And that what is present or on the horizon in our lives has come calling at the perfect time? Hindsight has offered all the clues I've ever needed to the magical ways our lives unfold.

Were it not for my first husband leaving, I would not have gone to graduate school, and most likely I would never have gotten sober. One thing has led to another from the moment he left, and the evolution of my life has been miraculous. And guess what? The same can be said for yours. Where you are at this moment is where you have been destined to be since an earlier time. You just didn't know it. You didn't see the signs. Enjoy them as you revisit your past. Let them enfold you in the peace you deserve.

What is hindsight showing you right now? Look long and hard. You will be amazed. Share what you see.

Let's write:

_____

_____

_____

_____

_____

_____

_____

_____

_____

_____

_____

_____

_____

Making Memories Is Another Way to Claim More Peace of Mind

As I have aged, I have thought far more frequently about the value of making memories while there is still time. Looking back through *Each Day a New Beginning*, I came across a line that drew me in. "I can make this day one to remember with fondness." You no doubt have made many fond memories. And today stands before you, wide open for you to make another fond memory or two.

Take a few moments to sift through earlier memories that are now calling to you. There is no time like the present to bathe yourself in a good memory. Good memories serve more than one purpose too. When we find ourselves in a situation that's troubling us, perhaps a person who might be getting under our skin; stopping for a moment to recall a fond memory can change our entire perspective. We can be at peace in that moment simply because we have remembered a fond memory. Right now is a good time to retrieve a good memory. You might need to use it tomorrow, or perhaps even today.

Here is the place and now is the time to share what one or two good memories might be. We never know for sure when we might need them to help us get over a troubling moment:

_____

_____

_____

_____

Switching Gears, But Not Away from Inner Peace

No one—no one at all we have met or will ever meet—is insignificant to our development as a human being on a journey to whatever the next stop is destined to be. Wow! What a realization. And what an idea to celebrate.

I surely can't speak for you, but when I was introduced to this idea a few decades ago I was skeptical. Back then I scoffed at a lot of things. I wasn't convinced there was a nonphysical presence in my life that had always been there guiding me, either. I surely didn't pay very close attention and made a lot of wrong turns.

But here I am today fully convinced that I am where I'm supposed to be and doing exactly what I have been called to do. The good news about this realization is that it means I can relax and trust that the nudges of guidance for where I need to go next will be felt. As the Big Book of Alcoholics Anonymous tells us: "We are always in the right place at the right time." That's pretty comforting to me. And hopefully it is to you as well. It does assure us of inner peace if we want to interpret it that way, and I do.

Is there something in these three paragraphs above that is speaking to you right now? If so, it would be a good time to let your inner voice guide your thoughts.

Please take this time to share those thoughts. There is no hurry:

_____

_____

_____

_____

The Importance of Those Who Came Before Us

Remembering grandparents might well bring a smile to your face. I certainly fall into that category. My mother's parents lived about thirty-five miles from where I grew up, and we saw them pretty often, even though thirty-five miles on a two-lane highway wasn't always a quick and easy trip in the early '40s.

But it always brought lots of laughter coupled with great memories. My grandmother was a wonderful cook. Her fried chicken, mashed potatoes, and gravy were the best. And my granddad was the candy bar distributor for all of Logansport, Indiana. You can imagine what that meant. We always came home with a big box of candy bars and very full stomachs.

Visiting them felt like a reprieve from my stormier household. And the real gift of their kindness was that it served as an example of how adults could be, both with each other and with all of the rest of us too. There was a feeling of genuine peace there, a pretty unfamiliar feeling to me.

We all need examples of how to become our better selves. Perhaps you have a forebear who played that role for you too. Think on this a few moments. And then share it here so you won't forget:

_____

_____

_____

_____

_____

_____

_____

_____

_____

_____

_____

_____

_____

_____

_____

_____

_____

(Remember, you too will serve in this role one day.)

Chapter 4

....

Tiny Rewards
Are Available in
Myriad Ways

The beauty of a tiny reward is simply that: It may be tiny, but often it's mighty. And for the most part, it may well be long-lasting. We are all deserving of rewards of one kind or another throughout our lives. We have worked hard, helped others along the way, and planned for the future. And those of us traversing this program of recovery have gone to great lengths to clean up our past.

Every one of us has been the recipient of many rewards throughout our lives, and deservedly so, oftentimes tucked in among some really painful experiences. Rewards have always been something we could count on, however, even though we may not have grown up with this awareness. Perhaps we have to reflect long and hard to remember what some of them were. Our own self-absorption may have stolen our attention away from them. But the rewards will remain in our memory bank, waiting for our rediscovery of them in recollection.

Let's just sit a spell right now and ponder about our lives up to this point. The rewards were many. Take some time to be embraced by them and grateful too. Then begin to share what some of them were. And as you are sharing, enjoy them once again like they are brand-new experiences.

It's time to write:

_____

_____

_____

_____

_____

_____

_____

_____

_____

_____

_____

_____

_____

_____

Selflessness Is Its Own Reward

Our rewards will keep coming; that's a fortunate fact of our lives.

But must we do something to assure that this is so? It's a worthy question, and one I've pondered over the years. I didn't come into the rooms of recovery in 1976 expecting rewards of any kind, and initially I didn't even recognize them.

Fortunately, hindsight teaches us so much. And listening to the wise words of others does too. And that's where our next opportunity might come from today. Just maybe we will be able to help someone else who is crossing our path recognize some rewards that have made a difference in his or her life. Not one of us has been overlooked in this department, but far too often we are too caught in the maelstrom of self-pity to see that we have been tapped on the shoulder by God, again and again.

How might we go about helping someone else today? And let's always remember that we are helped in the process too—always.

Can you begin thinking how to move forward with this idea? And can you see how it will reward you as well as the individual who receives your help?

Ponder, then write:

_____

_____

_____

_____

Finding Daily Rewards In Peaceful Pursuits

A tiny reward we can give ourselves is to do something that soothes us. Let's consider what ideas come to us.

I know I consider prayer and meditation very soothing, thus I do it every day. A long hot shower likewise helps me to release stress. Having a conversation with a dear friend in person or on the phone soothes me too, as does a walk with my husband Joe and our dog Nellie.

The small pleasures seem to count for even more as I age. Perhaps you are discovering this too. We each deserve rewards of some kind every day. Maybe we have grown accustomed to rewarding ourselves following a job well done. I know that after sitting at my computer most of the day, I consider watching a fun show on TV a reward. There is no one way to reward ourselves. We are free to choose whatever seems to call out to us, and no one is watching.

What are some of the things that call out to you as a reward after you have completed a necessary task or simply come to the end of your day? The sky is the limit.

Time to write:

_____

_____

_____

_____

_____

_____

_____

_____

_____

_____

Look back over your list. Is there something you haven't tried yet but that others have told you about that you'd like to put on a list for future consideration?

Share here:

_____

_____

_____

_____

_____

_____

_____

Become More Aware Of Catalyst Moments

Was there a turning point in your recovery journey that you ignored that might have rewarded you in a way you hadn't previously considered?

We've all had them. Don't fret, but do acknowledge it. Doing so will help you be more alert in the future. Turning points are gifts from God. The good news is that if ignored, they will come again. That's a promise!

Think about this idea. Recall the past. Enjoy it, even the forgotten turning point. What would you like to share about it now?

_____

_____

_____

_____

_____

_____

_____

_____

_____

_____

Savor What's Gained in Even Small Victories

One quote I love in *Each Day a New Beginning* is by Gertrude Stein: "It is a peaceful thing to be one succeeding." But how do we interpret this for ourselves, particularly as we look at the lives we have lived so far? That's the question we must consider.

It is a peaceful thing to have reached the conclusion of a task we have set for ourselves, whether it's a hefty one like writing an article or a poem that has called to us, or simply completing a homework assignment or something for the boss at work. As a matter of fact, each time we finish anything, it provides its own reward. Simply sweeping out the garage or another household chore also counts as a task we might need to complete.

Just knowing that we have come to the end of any endeavor gives us a reason for a respite. And that too is a reward in my book. In those moments we can be grateful for whatever help we feel we received from the Source that's always at hand to help us in every undertaking. Never do we work alone, regardless of how we define work.

I'm sure you have enjoyed the success of the proverbial job well done myriad times. What stands out in your mind as one of the takeaways? We all have many lessons learned in our lives, regardless of how many or few years we have lived. Surely some of them are truly precious. Now is a great time to recall what some of them were. They are well worth embracing. And there is no better time than now.

Let's write:

_____

_____

_____

_____

_____

_____

_____

_____

_____

_____

_____

_____

_____

_____

_____

_____

Cherish Wisdom

Grandparents are generally so wise, at least in hindsight. Remembering what they've shared can be a reward of its own special kind.

I remember my mother's parents with such fondness. They always greeted us with loving, open arms. I always knew when we drove to their home that we'd have a day of great food, lots of laughter, and even a frozen custard to top off the meal as there was an ice cream stand right across the street from their house.

And if there was enough time, we could count on my granddad taking us kids to the merry-go-round, which was not so very far down the street. What was especially lucky for us about that treat was that the fellow running the merry-go-round always made sure one of us got the gold ring because that meant my granddad would buy all of us tickets to ride a second time. For sure the fellow working knew a good thing when he saw it.

My grandparents seemed to know just what we needed, which was freedom from a generally tense household. A few hours of genuine fun offered a lot of relief and hope that under the right circumstances, life could be better.

Hopefully you have a memory of a situation in your past where a reward of some kind was offered at some point. Think a bit until a memory surfaces. Recalling those times in our lives is so good for our souls in any season.

It's time to daydream until a memory surfaces. Then it's time to share it here so you can "revisit" it later:

_____

_____

In Helping Others, We Help Ourselves

Offering help to someone else just might be the greatest of all rewards. What we give to others does indeed come back to us—multiplied tenfold.

The above idea, besides being true, is so powerful yet so very simple. I'm not suggesting that's the only reason for offering to help someone. On the contrary, deciding to be truly helpful every time we have an opportunity to do so is surely the loving thing to do. And there is no better way to journey through life than to be loving and kind. It promises peace of mind to us, and it promotes peace in the lives of others too. So many of those on this or another recovery path often yearn for peace. In the final analysis, being a conduit for peace is spreading good throughout the universe.

As I said in *Each Day a New Beginning*, "The need to grow, to change, to affect the world around us, is part of God's plan for each of us." And in every opportunity that may show up within each situation, we just might have the inclination to offer a reward to someone else. In so doing, we get hold of a rewarding experience for ourselves too. What a deal. Wouldn't you agree?

Can you conjure up a recollection where you were nearly instantly rewarded after offering your assistance to someone else? Watch for them. They are there.

Let's share a memory here:

_____

_____

_____

_____

_____

_____

_____

_____

_____

_____

_____

_____

_____

_____

_____

_____

_____

_____

_____

The Shape of Satisfaction

If you were invited to speak to a class of fourth graders about the topic of life's rewards, what might you tell them are the ones that still cling to your memory bank?

The point we want them to understand, of course, is that there is no one definition of what a reward looks like or feels like either. And we'd also want to get across to them that being young doesn't mean they haven't already received many rewards. Your job is to help them appreciate the various rewards they have received already, making a point of saying anything counts as one if they think of it that way.

What from your own experience would you use to help you connect with this group of youngsters? Where might you begin? What rewarding experiences that you have had in your life, particularly those you remember from your youth, would you share with them in your talk?

After some reflection, begin where it makes most sense to you:

_____

_____

_____

_____

_____

_____

_____

_____

_____

_____

_____

_____

_____

_____

_____

_____

_____

_____

_____

_____

_____

_____

_____

Change Can Be Its Own Reward

"When we are no longer able to change a situation, we are challenged to change ourselves."

—Viktor E. Frankl

Making a change, perhaps a new job, a new residence, or a new recovery meeting, might feel a bit challenging at first. The old experience was familiar, after all. But spreading our wings in a new direction can show us our capabilities; sometimes we discover strengths we never knew we had. And that's a reward we had never even considered.

And let's not forget that the biggest change for many of us was the decision to seek help and get sober. I went to my first AA meeting more than forty-eight years ago, and the desire to drink was lifted immediately. That was a huge change I had never before even considered making. Of course, that change was in God's plan for me all along, but I didn't know it at the time. In fact, I have experienced so many changes over these many years, and God was always a part of each one. The same is true for each one of you reading this book today as well.

Let's take a few moments and collect our thoughts about these changes. Every one of them was its own reward. I know my entire life from May 24, 1976 until today has been one reward after another. How about you? I think the time is right to make a list of all of these rewards. You will be dumbfounded. I was.

Make your list after some contemplation:

_____

_____

Cherish Each Moment's Unfolding

A thought I shared more than forty years ago in *Each Day a New Beginning* that I still live by is: "I will cherish every moment today. Each one is special and will not visit me again." We can only live one moment at a time. And we will be rewarded in some way within each moment. What a glorious realization—and how significant it makes each passing moment.

It's not always easy to appreciate each moment as it is slipping by. It's far too easy for most of us to still be lingering in the past or perhaps dreading the future. But if we dedicate ourselves to understanding that Right Now is all there is, that is in fact a joyous realization, one that eases our lives in so many ways. If we slip easily into each moment as it presents itself, we are free from worry and regret. Ah, freedom is an amazing reward.

How does this idea change your perspective? My hope is that you will find the comfort I have found. We all deserve greater peace. The angst too many of us have been living with can be a distant memory if we so choose.

How comfortable are you living one moment at a time? Is it a struggle? Can you see the rewards that are a certainty if you do wallow in the Now?

Think about your life and whatever struggles you may have with this idea and then prepare to write about them:

_____

_____

_____

_____

_____

_____

_____

_____

_____

_____

_____

_____

_____

_____

_____

_____

_____

_____

_____

Many tiny rewards have visited every one of us since we came into this recovery program. Let's simply reflect for the next few minutes and then share about them in any way that calls to you.

Are you ready to write?

_____

_____

_____

_____

_____

_____

_____

_____

_____

_____

_____

_____

Chapter 5

....

Meandering Can Lead Us to Many Good Places

Life is a compilation of our meanderings from one situation to another. And nary one of them is without its importance to the totality of our journey in this life. As I said in *Each Day a New Beginning*, "Today flows from yesterday, the day before, and the day before that. Tomorrow follows suit."

It's nice to know that we can count on the absolute truth of this statement. Nothing in our experience is wasted—ever. We need each situation, every person, and even every blunder along the way in order for us to experience the full expression of growth we are here to have. From my perspective, there's great freedom in knowing that. No need for regret. All is making its contribution and adding up to the life that is uniquely our own.

We have all meandered, and that's the good news. Perhaps we didn't previously look upon our meanderings as having purpose, but each one did. Let's take some time now to review our past. Were there *"side trips"* along the way that you can now see were absolutely necessary for you to end up where you are right now? Collect your thoughts for a time, make some notes if you need to organize recollections, and then prepare to write about these side trips that you can now see were so necessary for the person you have become.

Ready to write?

_____

_____

_____

_____

_____

_____

_____

_____

Would you care to comment on what was most valuable to you about this particular writing exercise?

_____

_____

_____

_____

_____

_____

_____

The Winding Way Forward

Meanderings are really for our enjoyment. They will take us to stopping off points we might have overlooked otherwise. As I said in *Each Day a New Beginning*, "I will look to this day with wonder and awe. Everything is okay." That's an idea we can take to the bank. No stopping off point was a mistake. In the final analysis, every detour was necessary for us to show up "on time" for the next encounter. What sweet joy there is in that realization.

What stopping off points can you now see were far from the waste of time you might have originally thought? I can surely see that some of my detours into relationships that were not healthy were actually leading me onto the path of recovery, first via Al-Anon and then AA. And without both programs, my life might have ended many years ago. Instead, I have met millions of you through my books and workshops over these forty-eight years. God always had a better plan than the one I had.

Perhaps you can see the truth of this idea in your journey too. Take a few moments now to reflect on your past, the detours as well as the surprises, and share how your life changed in the process of a few of these twists and turns.

Let's write:

_____

_____

_____

_____

_____

_____

_____

_____

_____

_____

Was there a right turn that you refused to make that you'd now like the chance to do over? What was it? How do you think it might have changed your peace of mind?

Share a bit here:

_____

_____

_____

_____

_____

_____

_____

_____

Trying Times Can Reveal the Presence of Your Higher Power

A quote from *Each Day a New Beginning* that I think should get our attention over and over is this: "Without challenges, we'd stagnate, enjoying life little, offering life nothing." Let's explore this idea carefully. I will share where I'm coming from first.

Before recovery I saw every challenge as "out to get me." I never considered them opportunities to move in a new direction, meet a new group of people, start a new job, or even move to a new location perhaps. Challenges were not my friends. They scared me. I was always certain they were more than I could handle. I never sought the help of a Higher Power then. Frankly, I wasn't a believer in God at that period of my life.

But guess what? God was there anyway, believing in me. That's the sweetest truth I have come to cherish since coming into the rooms of recovery. God didn't need me to believe in Him for Him to believe in me. What a gift. And for certain, what has been true for me has been true for you as well. Without a doubt!

Take some time here to just soak in that realization. God believed in you all along. Can you see any evidence of His presence when you quiet your mind of everything else?

Take all the time you need and then write about your awarenesses. He was there—always:

_____

_____

_____

_____

_____

_____

_____

_____

_____

What's the most amazing awareness you uncovered that takes you
by surprise?

_____

_____

_____

_____

_____

_____

_____

Meandering

Meandering doesn't always mean the same thing to everyone. For some, it might mean wasting time, not really moving forward in a "thoughtful, scripted fashion." For others it might mean daydreaming, not ever leaving the confines of one's office or front porch. Personally, I like to think of meandering as allowing my mind to direct me wherever it wants to go, perhaps introducing me to an idea that is altogether new, or pulling me back into an earlier memory that's not really done with me yet. Meandering is the pathway to discovery, and that can mean many things.

Meandering is whatever you might choose for it to be. Now, is there any one of these examples that appeals to you or is similar to how you define meandering? If not, what's your definition, and what have your meanderings taught you? What have you learned about your past, or even your life right here and now?

After some quiet pondering, please share what's on your mind about meandering and how it fits into your life:

_____

_____

_____

_____

_____

_____

And Then That Time...

Meandering through our own minds, which comes easier to some of us than meandering through the park, might reintroduce us to awarenesses we'd actually rather not recall. Personally, I consider those recollections far from accidental—quite the opposite, in fact.

I think we may all have past experiences that haunt us for one reason or another. I know I do. One I'll share now is that when I was an undergraduate at Purdue University, my drinking was out of control. And one night, a number of us ended up going to a party at a young couple's apartment. I have no recollection who they were. I only remember that they'd recently had a new baby. And my recollection, one I'm not proud of, is that I made out with the husband when everyone else was in the living room partying. Was I even ashamed at the time? It's surely doubtful. But it happened, and I've never forgotten it.

I think a recollection like this is good when we are "meandering" because it reminds us of our humanity. It also gives us the evidence we might need not to repeat that kind of poor behavior again. And best of all, it allows us the much-needed opportunity to forgive ourselves.

Perhaps your meanderings won't dig up something as unseemly as mine did, but does anything come to mind that you wish you hadn't done? Remember though, we were forgiven by God just as quickly as we committed the wrongdoing. There is no condemnation ever from our Higher Power. We do enough of that ourselves. And now it's time to practice forgiveness of ourselves.

What has come to your mind as the result of your meanderings that you know it's time to be done with? After some reflection, please share:

_____

_____

_____

_____

_____

_____

_____

_____

_____

_____

_____

_____

Is there anything that took you a bit by surprise as you delved into this "assignment?"

_____

_____

_____

_____

_____

_____

_____

_____

_____

_____

_____

_____

Nothing Is Wasted

Nothing is ever wasted: No thought. No encounter. No detour. Obviously this means no time we have spent meandering through our lives, whether only in our minds or in the neighboring park, is wasted either. Something was always calling to us—many somethings, in fact. Can you sit a spell and allow your memory to recall a few of these?

When you feel ready, please share them here for your own edification and joy. Particularly your joy:

_____

_____

_____

_____

_____

_____

_____

_____

No Time Like the Present

There is simply no time like the present for gathering all the gifts from our past that may have gone unappreciated in the passing years. Don't you think it's time to "reopen" those gifts? I do.

You may need to "meander" for a spell through your own life to catch a glimpse of some truly special ones. You have all the time you need. No one is timing you.

Please write when ready:

_____

_____

_____

_____

_____

_____

_____

_____

_____

Wandering Down Memory Lane

Wandering through our memories is a real luxury. I'm so glad you think you deserve this special time. And as we wander, we will come upon events we had forgotten entirely about. I'm pretty sure of that. One way to wander is to go through a collection of old pictures. They will transport you down memory lane pretty quickly.

Reading old journals does the trick too. Why do we even need to bother, you might be wondering. I think the primary reason for this exploration is to measure just how far we have come. And frankly, I think certain memories we may meander by are so very worthy of a second or even a third look. They contributed so much. No doubt we didn't realize at the time of the experience just what significance it had in the overall unfolding of our lives. But as I've said previously, not a single experience failed to make its mark. And each recollection of it is likewise making its mark too.

For sure we will never remember all of the trigger events, no matter how many pictures we look at or journal entries we read. But they will wait for our attention to them at a later date. They won't leave us—ever. A lot like God.

Care to begin recounting some memories? Here's where:

_____

_____

_____

_____

_____

_____

_____

_____

_____

_____

Is there any one theme you can see in hindsight that emerges more than once? If so, you may want to write about that too:

_____

_____

_____

_____

_____

_____

_____

_____

_____

Impossible May Just Be a Matter of Opinion

Perhaps you want to take a short break from meandering and memories. What is calling you right now? If nothing seems to be coming to mind, let me suggest a quote from *Each Day a New Beginning* that might be worthy of your attention.

"You must do the thing you think you cannot do."

—Eleanor Roosevelt

I've loved this quote ever since first reading it. Even though I wasn't aware of it until I was in my thirties, I realized the idea itself had been expressed in my life over and over since childhood. My family of origin was very focused on not making mistakes so I was challenged to be perfect, an impossibility of course. But I was hypervigilant in my effort to be as near perfect as possible. The upside was that I succeeded at many things I may not have even tried if my upbringing had been different.

As I grew older, I continued to set my sights pretty high. While in high school, I worked twenty hours a week at a large department store while maintaining an A average. Even though I had my problems with alcoholism a bit later in life, I still set goals and succeeded at them, over and over. It was as though my inner voice was always repeating the quote by Eleanor Roosevelt, even throughout my doctoral program. Being inspired by someone can move us forward in a nearly magical way. I experienced this again and again. And now I also have forty-eight years of recovery in Alcoholics Anonymous as a result of "doing that which I think I cannot do."

How about you? Is there something you'd like to share along these lines?
Now is the perfect time:

_____

_____

_____

_____

_____

_____

_____

And if nothing about this idea appealed to you, choose one that does and
open your heart here:

_____

_____

_____

_____

_____

_____

_____

Little Strokes Fell Great Oaks

A thought I had while writing *Each Day a New Beginning* was this: "Our lives unfold in small measures, just as small as they need to be for our personal comfort... We are on a pathway to goodness."

And I still live by these words more than forty years later. The experiences we need come to us incrementally so that we can grow incrementally too. And if we revisit our past, meander through it as we have been doing in these last few exercises, we can see the multitude of incremental opportunities that we have been privy to over the years.

The interesting thing, I think, is that at the time, most of them slipped by nearly unnoticed as the necessary experiences we needed to go where we were ultimately headed. One just melded into the next. But giving a second look offers us so much. Seeing the perfection in how our lives actually did unfold is the gift of God for which we might well have failed to be grateful.

Of course, not every experience felt great in its moment; for instance, my first husband's infidelities and then his decision to leave for another woman. However, as I have mentioned previously, that opened many doors for me, and today I sit here writing my thirty-first book after earning a doctorate and being sober forty-eight years. And I have him to thank for it—him and God, of course.

What about you? You can point to many successes that came your way just because... Would you care to delve into a few of them now?

Here's where you can:

_____

_____

_____

_____

_____

_____

_____

_____

_____

_____

_____

_____

_____

Go at Your Own Pace

Even though the past is gone and unchangeable—as the saying goes, "Even God can't change the past"—it has showered us with morsels galore that have guided us for all the years we have been alive. And as I've said repeatedly, not every morsel "tasted good" at the time we swallowed it. But it was a necessary ingredient for the full development of who we are now.

As I've also been saying for these last few writing exercises, you may find that meandering in and around them now can be spellbinding, shocking, completely surprising, or may result in a state of disbelief about what these morsels actually were offering us, then and now. But continuing to integrate what we are realizing from those experiences is worth the effort. We are becoming even better people as a result, and definitely more knowledgeable about the purpose of our journey here.

It may well be time to take a deep breath. We don't always want to actually accept what we know to have been true. That's okay; it's normal. Let's take a rest. Review these morsels in whatever way appeals to you. Then rest some more if that's your preference. I have no expectations of you here. You are on your own journey, learning whatever you want to learn. And you are the only observer too. What you write is for you only. When you write is your choice.

When you are ready, here is the place to share:

_____

_____

_____

_____

Chapter 6

God Journeyed with Us—Always

Our journey has been amazing in every regard. It hasn't skipped an experience we have been meant to have. And that will always be true because God is and was always present to walk us through everything. This will remain a fact of our lives—forever. How lucky can you and I be?

In the past, we may have wanted to put an experience on hold for a time, and that was okay. If one comes our way that we don't feel ready for now or in the future, it will wait for us. By revisiting our past, we can see where this was evident, in fact. The good news is none of us were ever forced into any experience until we were ready to incorporate it into our lives. We can count on this remaining true from here forward too.

Do you see some experiences now that you did postpone for a time, or some that you wish you had postponed? These recollections have a lot to teach us. At the top of the list is that no experience was ever superfluous, no matter when we agreed to walk through it. It was always woven perfectly into what preceded it and what followed it too.

On innumerable occasions I didn't really want my life to change. I actually thought that being married to an unfaithful husband or sitting on a bar stool after a long day in graduate school were just fine as they were. How much was soon to change in both instances. And the change was always right around the corner. How glad I am that my life was destined for a different journey, sudden though each change may have felt at the time.

Surely you can relate. Not a one of us has traveled a perfectly straight line to where we are right now. No matter where you are on your journey, you have traveled long and far enough now to see what you really couldn't see when trapped in the maelstrom of a life moving forward. Was there something you wanted to put on hold? Anything? And where do you see now that God was leading you, with or without your approval initially? It was the destination that was always yours to experience. And you arrived, not a minute too soon or too late. But it had to be.

What is coming to your mind right now regarding all of the above? Take a few quiet moments to reflect and then write to your heart's content in any direction that you feel pulled to go:

_____

_____

_____

_____

_____

_____

_____

_____

_____

The important consideration here is what are you learning about yourself, your past, or where you want to go in the future? These questions are worthy of contemplation. Take all the time you need and then share whatever comes to you:

_____

_____

_____

_____

_____

_____

_____

_____

_____

_____

A Deep Breath

The assurance that God is and was always within, traveling every step with us, changes the game plan, doesn't it? I didn't come into the rooms of AA and Al-Anon a believer, however. But how glad I am that I have had a change of mind.

As I said in *Each Day a New Beginning*: "A deep breath invites the inner strength to move through me. I will feel the exhilaration of God's power." And that feeling will never leave us if, and it's a big if, you and I always remember to take that deep breath.

No doubt you can look over the years you have lived and be astounded by the myriad times you did have a conscious realization of God's presence. For some of us, it may number in the hundreds. For many of us, no doubt, far less. But He was there, nonetheless, whether we noticed or not. That's the really neat thing about God. He doesn't require our attention for Him to stay present. As a good friend of mine says, "God is not codependent."

Recalling His presence is simply good for your sense of well-being and purpose, I think. It's kind of like reviewing an insurance policy. When you see the frequency of His showing up, it relieves you of your concern regarding the future, if you have some.

It's time now for you to do your thinking and then writing. It will be a great reminder of just how committed God is to your life. Frankly, it can't be any other way. He is within you all of the time.

Here is the place:

_____

_____

_____

_____

_____

_____

_____

_____

_____

_____

_____

_____

_____

_____

_____

A Change of Pace

What is crying to be looked at in greater detail that you haven't been prompted to examine yet? Remember, *this workbook is yours*. I'm only trying to offer some guidance for where you might want to go with your thoughts regarding the past or potential plans for the future. I may not be hitting those areas that are calling to you to be written about. So you have all the permission you need to call a halt to the writing I've been suggesting here and go wherever you want for the next writing session. To reiterate, this is your workbook. This is your life you are reviewing. I give you all the freedom you need or want to go next wherever your thoughts take you.

Here is the place and the time is now:

_____

_____

_____

_____

_____

_____

_____

_____

Spell Out What Would Make Your Dreams Come True

Isn't it fun to know that you can make of this workbook experience whatever you want it to be?

Not much in our lives is so independent of what others might want us to do and think. But here you are free, completely free to say and write whatever calls to you about your past, the impending future, or specific dreams you might have. There is *no one to say no to you! No one.*

It reminds me of the freedom I felt when I was writing *Each Day a New Beginning.* Of course, I didn't know at that time that it would ever be a book that would land in the hands of others. I was simply conversing with God on paper, using a legal pad and pen, in fact. I was desperately seeking some sense of His presence. Others of my friends seemed to have it, but it was so fleeting for me. I felt He was offering me guidance with every word I wrote. And He was assuring me with every word that He was right there and would always remain so. I just couldn't remember except when I was sitting in that old beat-up recliner.

Never have I felt like I was the sole author of that book—or of any other book I have written, for that matter. What an amazing journey my writing has been. And I hope you as well are having an amazing experience with what you are being inspired to write in these pages.

Let's take a brief right turn and consider for a moment an activity or adventure or new direction for your life that you've thought about daring to do. And let's remember that God travels with you everywhere you go—absolutely everywhere. Does remembering this give you the courage to forge ahead?

What would that adventure or new direction be? This is the place to flesh it out. There is only you, your dream, and God's presence. Why not have some fun with the idea and see how it feels as you write about it? In particular, see where the dream takes you. And don't hesitate to write what is really there to be written.

No one is watching—except God, of course, and He has already said yes. Go for it. Here is the place and now is the time:

_____

_____

_____

_____

_____

_____

_____

_____

_____

_____

_____

Implementing Change

"As we think, so we are." What a powerful idea this is. And when the thought is negative, we might feel penned in. Fortunately, you and I always have the capacity to change our minds. And with God's help, it's not so very hard to change our minds. What is hard for some of us, though, is staying committed to the change. Practice, practice, practice: That's the key.

Is there some change you have felt called to make but simply haven't been committed to yet? There is no better time than now. And it's really not that hard. Perhaps you need some time before you begin writing to sort through who and where you are right now. That's usually the first step. And the second one is to ask: Where and who would you rather be?

Let's ponder first. Then let's write:

_____

_____

_____

_____

_____

_____

_____

Now let's imagine this new you in a typical situation that might present itself. How do you navigate the experience? That's the real test.

Share that realization here:

_____

_____

_____

_____

_____

_____

_____

_____

_____

_____

_____

_____

The Road to Faith

Today I am reflecting on something I wrote in *Each Day a New Beginning*: "As we look toward the hours ahead, we can be thankful that we need be concerned with only a single day's worth of hours. No more."

Because we have been promised that our spiritual Companion is by our side every step of the way, not just for these few hours, but for every hour that remains to us in this lifetime, we can breathe a long sigh of relief. Of course, we have to believe this as our truth in order to fully reap the benefits of it. And not everyone has embraced this idea. Perhaps you didn't embrace it initially either. Or you may still struggle at times to let it comfort you. I well remember the struggle I had, one that I occasionally still have.

When I first entered the rooms of AA, as I mentioned earlier in this workbook, I was a nonbeliever. I'd sit in meetings and feel a sense of comfort from what others said, and I'd thoroughly enjoy the many hours we spent together before, during, and following the meetings; but then I'd go home and be anxious once again. I simply couldn't maintain the comfort I'd feel in the presence of my believing friends.

Thank goodness that eventually changed, but the change wasn't immediate. In fact, it didn't happen until I began to connect with the God of my understanding through writing.

We all have to find our own way to connect, don't we? Fortunately for me I had learned in graduate school that writing was my pathway to peace of mind. I didn't know at that time, of course, that it would open the door for the work I was destined to do for the rest of my life. Only God was privy to that understanding back then. All I knew while in school was that something magical happened when I sat down to write. I felt transported to a place where comfort was as present as my right hand while I wrote. That same magic was present as I began my daily communication with God while sitting in my old brown recliner in my upstairs study, with pen in hand and legal pad on my lap.

We all have to find our way to God before we can begin counting on His constant presence. It was always there, though. He didn't need our attention for Him to stick around—not at all. Weren't we lucky?

Do you remember when you first realized how present God was in your life? Maybe it was in your childhood if you were lucky, or your teens, or maybe not until early recovery. Being grateful for that recollection is what I want you to concentrate on right now. It was of paramount importance. And continuing to remember and then embrace the knowledge of His presence changed everything for you, as it did for me, and this remains one of the most important gifts to be grateful for.

(Perhaps some of you haven't yet had this awareness, but you will have it at some point. Please anticipate how this awareness might change how you experience your life: Could it give you self-assurance? Might it calm your emotions at those times fear has gripped you? Please describe how your life might change as a result of knowing that God was and always will be present.)

Please take some time now to remember how you made that connection the first time, and how you have maintained it too. Meditate if that helps. Perhaps even take a walk. Then savor the memory before writing about it.

Now it's time to write:

_____

_____

_____

_____

The Island of Aloneness

We are never alone; that's a fact. However, have you ever felt abandoned by God? Feeling that sense of total isolation isn't all that unusual. Fortunately, for most of us, it's short-lived; but when it befalls us, the fear can be debilitating.

I well remember the times I felt completely isolated. Even in the midst of my friends in AA, I'd sometimes feel like I couldn't reach them, that I was invisible, separate, and would never be connected to them again.

What brings a feeling like this on? That's the million-dollar question, and I have come to believe there is actually a simple answer. It's our codependence. We want to be the focus of everyone else's life. And when others go about living as they must, we feel pushed aside, separate, and discarded. "Hey, what about me?" And the fear of isolation heightens.

What we must never forget, however, is that we are never alone; we are never pushed aside by God. We are always in the right place at the right time having the experience for growth that we need—every time! As I said in *Each Day a New Beginning*, "We are moving toward greater understanding of life's mysteries with each experience." This is the absolute truth we can always count on.

Hopefully, what I have shared here has tickled your memory somewhat. Have you ever felt pushed aside? Have you ever felt forgotten by God? Share your recollections here, and also share what new understanding you might now have about those experiences.

It's time to write whenever you are ready:

_____

_____

_____

_____

_____

_____

_____

_____

_____

_____

_____

_____

_____

_____

_____

_____

_____

_____

Inviting the Help of Your Higher Power

I'm often reminded of Anne Frank's connection to God and the hope of survival expressed through her writing. Although she didn't survive her traumatic life—she actually died of typhus while in a concentration camp—her words have given hope to others for the many decades since her death.

We simply don't always understand what we have been called to do. Perhaps the best we can know is to follow that inner guidance, whatever it is, just as Anne did. God has a plan for each of us. And the pathway to our own peace is to agree to that plan, knowing that others will be lovingly impacted as well. Anne followed her plan, and we have been privy to her life, her strength, and her love and kindness as the result of it. That she never lost hope is perhaps the greatest of all lessons for the rest of us.

You have surely faced challenges. We all have. Most likely yours have not been of the same variety as Anne Frank's, but they might have been equally traumatic to you at that time. But you are on the other side now.

What did you learn from the most challenging experience you ever had? Have you had an opportunity to share that experience with someone else so that she or he may achieve some clarity about something they are living through? That help and clarity surely are what God hopes for us to find. Wouldn't you agree?

Think a spell about the challenges in your life. What comes to mind as the most sought-after solution? Did God help you navigate it? He is always ready to do so, you know. After you have given some time to this contemplation, please share. It's good for you to remember the details. Challenges are a fact of our lives. And referring back to how we handled them in the past makes any current situation less taxing to our peace of mind.

After reflecting a bit, share here:

_____

_____

_____

_____

_____

_____

_____

_____

_____

_____

_____

_____

_____

_____

_____

The Sum of Our Experiences

"We must not let a single moment go by unnoticed." Once again I've turned to *Each Day a New Beginning* for a prompt for you to explore more about yourself. That's what this workbook is designed to do for you, after all. Unexamined lives prevent us from knowing who we really are, and if you don't know who you are, you'll not master the lessons you were born to learn.

A belief that I have grown to cherish is that we do come into this earthly existence with "assignments." And the multitude of people with whom we cross paths are likewise on assignment. We intersect, as we must; and the intersection is for the sole purpose of allowing both of us to learn what we came here to learn. Maybe this idea is a bit of a stretch for you. It was for me when I was first introduced to it in a book by Caroline Myss titled *Sacred Contacts*, but in time, it comforted me. It meant I was always where I needed to be, with the very opportunity for which I was ready at that moment.

Admittedly, not all opportunities please us when they first come calling, and we can bypass them for a time. They will simply call to us again. The real point is that whatever the opportunity is or was, we needed to walk through it to become the people you and I are now.

Perhaps you are recalling some of these opportunities that you were slow to embrace. We have all had them. But in time, we will see what we have needed to see all along. At least, that has been my experience. Hindsight is so revealing.

Take some time now to review some opportunities that you were slow to embrace. What have you learned about them and yourself? Where did the opportunity ultimately lead you? Can you now see its value? Can you see how it has fit into your overall tapestry?

Let's take time to ponder and then write:

Sheltered by His Wings

"Sometimes the things that frighten you the most can be the biggest sources of strength."

—Iris Timberlake

My aunt Iris was a tiny woman who probably weighed no more than eighty-five pounds, but she was strong in so many ways. She owned a gift store in Logansport, Indiana, with my Uncle Grover. Together they were a mighty force in that town and met many challenges with fortitude and faith.

That's what you and I have to do too. We have to trust that all is well, that it always has been and will remain so forever. And why is that? Because nothing is outside of God's constant regard.

Hopefully you can see how true this was as you look to yesteryear. A lot happened in your life that didn't feel great at the time. Right? Perhaps, like me, you had a cheating spouse; or a health challenge that caught you by surprise; or a job loss that threw you for a loop. But the truth of the matter is that there actually were no surprises in our lives. We might have been surprised in that moment. But guess who was always there to help us meet the situation?

Life is about change, but there is one thing in our lives, yours and mine, that is, always was, and will always be constant. And you know what that is. I know you do.

How has the constancy of God's presence kept you on track to move forward even when you were uneasy? Don't be ashamed if you have forgotten on occasion. We have all forgotten in the fear of the moment. But remembering to pause and come back to an awareness of our truth quiets our beating heart. God is here now. Always!

Celebrating that truth will keep it alive for you. And that means it will undergird our existence for as long as we live.

When was the most recent time you were able to rest more easily because you remembered the presence of God? Please share your recollection here. Writing about it will help you to remember to opt for this same opportunity in the future too.

Please share your recollection here:

_____

_____

_____

_____

_____

_____

_____

_____

Experiential Assignments by Divine Design

"Our interests entice us to live up to God's expectations."

When I penned *Each Day a New Beginning*, I certainly never thought that my love of writing was inspired by God for a purpose far bigger than any dream I'd ever had. My fondness for writing was born in graduate school, but at that time I never would have guessed God had a far different plan for me and my writing. We are often the last to know.

So seldom do we know in the midst of the journey exactly where we are heading. And frankly, I think that makes each moment of each day pretty intriguing. Not knowing each step of the way where we will actually arrive, but trusting, as we finally must, that God is with us makes the final destination worth waiting for.

By now, you have surely had a destination that you didn't know was on your horizon. Depending on your age, it may well be one of many destinations you will have. The point is that the "script" has been written. Your job is to continue speaking your lines at the right time and to the right people, and you will assuredly be prompted to do so—never fear.

It's kind of fun looking at our lives from this perspective, I think. Don't you agree? We are scheduled to be doing what we are doing. And as I have indicated at an earlier time, you can bypass the schedule temporarily, but each "assignment" will show up again to be addressed at a later time. You can choose the time to address it, but you can't bypass it forever. Your ultimate destination needs every assignment.

I think it's enlightening to review those assignments we may have bypassed for a time. I surely had some in my first marriage. I had multiple opportunities to learn about codependency and the ways it had ravaged my life. The opportunities rolled around again before and during my second marriage. But I met them in a far different way. I'm pretty certain that you can relate. After all, if you are reading this book, we are not all that different, you and I.

Your interests were, and will continue to be, very much in keeping with God's plan for your life. You may not have considered that to be the underlying fact of the direction you have been heading, but knowing it now should make many things clear. Why not stop for a few moments and reflect on this information? God always knew where He wanted you to go. You may have resisted, but guess what? Where you are right now pretty well fits His picture. Perhaps it's time to rejoice.

Think about the picture of your life from your current perspective. What do you see? Are you happy with what you see?

Share your thoughts here please:

_____

_____

_____

_____

_____

_____

_____

The Simplest Purpose

Our ultimate job in this life is actually pretty simple; it's to be kind and loving. As I said in *Each Day a New Beginning*, "Each and every expression of love I offer today will make smooth another step I take in this life." Pretty simple. Wouldn't you agree?

How you and I can complicate our lives. I so well remember how I drove myself crazy trying to discern what God's will for me was when I first came into the rooms of AA. Simply to be loving and kind never crossed my mind. I figured it had to be far more specific and complicated; perhaps it was for me to move across the country or go to a foreign land to be a volunteer. If only I had asked God for help to understand, my early years might have been far more peaceful.

Maybe you didn't struggle as I did. In fact, I hope you didn't. But how did you navigate those times as you sorted out God's will for you? Were you one of the lucky ones who always knew that God was present to guide and comfort you? Or were you more like me and came to understand that presence slowly, very slowly?

It's a good time to reflect on that period of our lives. What were you in tune with? What did you still need to embrace? There was no right or wrong way to move into greater understanding. Whatever your way was, it was the right way for you.

Take some time now to enjoy revisiting whatever your process was. And then share your recollections here:

_____

_____

Chapter 7

....

Inch by Inch Is Still Forward Motion

What good news it is to be reminded that small, kind acts are every bit as valuable as great big ones. Each act is moving us forward. Mother Teresa famously said, "Not all of us can do great things, but we can do small things with great love." And a small thing can be just as simple as a smile, can't it? Or a nod of the head toward a stranger in a moment of silence. Each action any one of us takes that is loving is making our universe a far better place. I believe this wholeheartedly. I hope you do too.

There was a time in my life when I always waited for the other person to make the kind gesture. I don't think it was about being shy, but rather fearful that I wasn't worth another being paying attention to me. My codependency ruled my life. I needed your attention, kind attention in fact, to believe that I mattered at all. I lived in the hell of codependency for many years. Al-Anon has now transformed my life and how I navigate every encounter I have on a daily basis. Your approval or disapproval need never define me nor determine my reaction to anything. And that's been a miraculous change.

Perhaps you never were troubled by codependency. Regardless, the opportunity to recognize the value of small gestures of kindness in helping us to move forward inch by inch in a peaceful way is well worth our consideration. Remember, it's not about making great leaps forward. It's about helping to elevate the vibration of the universe. And both you and I can have an impact every moment we are alive. There is nothing mysterious about it, nor is it a difficult choice. It's saying yes to kindness. That's all. Personally, I think that's quite enough.

Where do you align yourself with this idea? Are you conscious of always trying to offer the hand of kindness in your encounters? What have you discovered to be the most common response to your gesture? Has that convinced you to keep trying?

Give some consideration to all of these questions and to Mother Teresa's quote. Where do you see yourself? Can you see any opportunities for change?

It's time to write:

_____

_____

_____

_____

_____

_____

_____

_____

Stitches in the Tapestry

When I think about the idea of moving forward inch by inch, I'm reminded of something I said in *Each Day a New Beginning* more than forty years ago: "In my personal drama, I am sharing the stage with everyone else I encounter today." That means each one of us is moving inch by inch and quite deliberately, whether we realize it or not. What an amazing and hefty bit of truth that is.

Did you ever stop to consider the absolute necessity of meeting all of the people you have met up until this point? Probably not, but with each of them there was a reason for you to come together to learn from each other something of importance.

Hopefully you haven't forgotten what I shared about Caroline Myss' perspective that we meet those we "agreed" to meet before ever awakening to this earthly existence. If you take a hard look at all you have learned and the people who helped you learn those lessons, perhaps including lessons you didn't like at the time, you will see the wisdom of her perspective.

I'm pretty sure you, like me, see a long list of people and previous lessons when you look to your past. Some of those lessons probably threw you for a loop. Others you may have loved. All of them were necessary, however. And there will be many more to come.

It's time to revisit those memories. As I said, some may not have been easy lessons but they did move you forward, inch by inch, and it's time to pay them homage. It would be a good idea to remember an incident, along with the person and the lesson involved, and see how it has wedged itself into the picture that is you today. You might be pleasantly surprised.

Take time to reflect… What are a few of those experiences and the "teachers" involved? Time now to write:

_____

_____

_____

_____

_____

_____

_____

_____

_____

_____

_____

_____

_____

_____

If You Could Visit Any Memory, What Would You Find?

We are always moving forward; even when it feels like we are standing quite still, time has moved us forward. Take this into account as you share what is calling to *you* to write about next; delving into whatever seems important to you at this moment is indeed what needs to be shared now. It's certain that I'm not going to think of everything that might matter to you, and as I said earlier, this workbook is about you and your awarenesses. My part has simply been to try and tickle your memory a bit. Perhaps I have missed the boat entirely in some respects, so please accept my invitation to bring up for yourself what matters to you. You aren't being graded, after all. This is not a college class but a memoir of sorts. It's for your eyes only unless you decide you want to share parts of it with others.

I know it's been really important for me to revisit all the little ways my life has been helped by an unexpected introduction here or a seeming failure there. Everything played its part in the drama that was unfolding, the drama that I was the star of.

Your own drama has been every bit as purposeful as mine. Take a long look. Are there any tiny scenes that ultimately opened the curtain to a whole new act? Those are the fun ones to revisit. Remember, every inch of your life mattered and always will.

What are some of those things you can now see really mattered even though you paid little attention to them at the time of their occurrence? Perhaps it's time to pay them homage by writing about them here after some reflection.

Is it time to write?

_____

_____

_____

_____

_____

_____

_____

_____

_____

_____

_____

_____

_____

_____

_____

_____

Practice Makes Progress

One way to look at how we have moved forward inch by inch is by reviewing our strengths—our inner assets. Choose one that you know you are in the midst of strengthening and practice it until it becomes a solid habit. It won't happen overnight.

And choose one that needs a hefty dose of practicing again because you have gotten a bit rusty. With more practice, it can once again become second nature to you. Nothing happens quickly, and most changes in us aren't all that easily made, let alone mastered.

Inch by inch, one day at a time, we do move forward, however. How lucky you and I are that we are in a program that clearly emphasizes we can only focus on today. And that fact will never change for you—or me.

Intentionally evaluating my inner strengths has become even more pleasurable as I have aged. As a younger woman, I was often way too focused on all that was wrong with me. I didn't grow up feeling very secure; thus, I felt I fell pretty short on strong points. It took a number of years in recovery for me to comfortably assess how accomplished I was in some areas. When one's family of origin is always quick to point out one's failings, it becomes second nature to allow those shortcomings to take center stage, even as an adult.

But that has changed. It's my hope that has changed for you too. Every one of us has lots of inner assets, and those inner qualities can ease our forward movement on this path with the necessary sense that anything that comes our way can be handled, and in time, handled with ease.

It's a good time right now for you to reflect on more recent situations that you handled with ease but that might have caused you to take a tumble in the past. There have been some, I'm sure of it. And every one of them brought you closer to who you were born to be.

The realization that you and I were born to be someone in particular is a pretty awesome idea from my perspective. I sure didn't live in the embrace of this awareness in my earlier years. Had I known the truth about my journey, I could have rested more easily. I'm guessing this might be true for you too. But now you also have a chance to revisit some of those so very necessary situations in your past. What were the gifts? They were there for sure.

After some moments of quiet reflection, take the next few moments to write about some of those gifts:

_____

_____

_____

_____

_____

_____

_____

_____

_____

_____

_____

Unfolding Memories

Inching right along is a manageable way to both live in the present and to review the past too. Whether we realized it or not, our lives were always lived moment by moment, an inch at a time, you might say. Quite likely you were often caught up in the past or the future. I know I was. However, this moment is all we can be sure of. Darn it!

But taking it an inch at a time is the easiest way to capture the picture of who you and I were. There is no way to absorb the totality of who we were in a glimpse. It's like looking at the collection of snapshots in an old box or paging through pictures on our phones. Looking at the past inch by inch can best be compared to taking each photo and savoring it for the memory it continues to hold for us now. It's like repeating a favorite vacation, but this time, you can linger with each moment even longer than the experience originally lasted.

Time is such an interesting phenomenon. Its passage so often literally goes unnoticed. Yet at other times it drags, and we can't focus anywhere but on how slowly the minutes seem to be slipping by. Remember your childhood and how eager you were for summer vacation, for instance? When we revisit the past through the help of a photo or a conversation, it may seem like the experience was in a different lifetime. Yet we lived from whatever moment or collection of moments that was then to where we sit now, moving inch by inch.

How lucky you and I are that we have the gift of a memory to savor whatever has gone before. And any memory you might be making today will await your recall of it at a future time. Our memories may grow dim, but for most of us, it takes only a picture in a box or on a phone to bring the experience back again.

Is there a particular memory you are savoring today? It could be a recent one or one long gone. Whatever it is, it has stayed in your mind for a reason. Embrace it once again here and now:

_____

_____

_____

_____

_____

_____

_____

_____

_____

_____

_____

_____

_____

Where to Now?

Since this chapter is about inching forward, perhaps we should consider where we want to inch forward to next. Reviewing our past is educational, for sure, but charting our future and even setting a few goals is a very worthy activity. Now we need to remember that our goals may not be consistent with those set by God for our journey. In fact, my goals in life didn't even come close to what God had in store for me.

Maybe yours were closer to the mark than mine were, but whether God's goals for us match our own momentary goals or not isn't all that important. It's good for us to take a full measure of ourselves and contemplate just where we may see ourselves on the next leg of our journey.

The good news always is that God will get your attention if you are headed in the wrong direction. We need not worry about that. And His plans will dovetail beautifully with the plans He has for your fellow travelers too. It's like we are all playing a particular instrument in God's orchestra and He is the conductor. All you and I have to do is take our assigned seats and the score will appear on the music stand before us.

Our past goal-setting wasn't wasted effort, however. It kept us engaged with life, and our intention to connect more fully with our path didn't go unnoticed by the God of our understanding. No doubt most of us had to make a detour to follow God's plan, but the destination always awaited us, which is particularly obvious in hindsight.

Take a gander at your own collection of destinations up to now. Perhaps you landed a job you had no expectation of ever holding. Guess what? God knew it was perfect for you. Or maybe you made a new friend at the gym and the two of you have encouraged each other to stay committed to working out when you really wanted to toss in the towel.

Or just maybe you met the person you may well spend the rest of your life with. Think that's an accident? Think again. Remember, there are no accidents in God's world, and that includes our world too.

Might you take time now for reflecting on where you want to inch to next? Just as long as you remember that God may change your route, you can begin charting the course. You will end up where you need to be, and that's a promise. I've loved reviewing the tapestry of my life to see where God wanted me that I hadn't planned on going. It was always to a far better place too. I think you will be able to see where God intervened in your life as well, and always for the better.

What are some of those "divine interventions" in your life? They are worthy of your appreciation. After drawing them to mind, write about them here:

_____

_____

_____

_____

_____

_____

_____

_____

Inch by Inch Is a Good Thing

The idea that our lives inch forward rather than leap too quickly into uncharted territory is quietly calming, isn't it? Too much too soon can cause us to feel anxious and uncertain, unless we have a constant sense of God's unwavering presence. Perhaps you do have that sense, and if so, how lucky you are. Many of us on this recovery path were hesitant to give our lives over completely to a God we may not have understood; at least, that was one of the struggles I had.

I actually experienced more than just a few years on a search for the God many others seemed to so easily trust in. And as I mentioned earlier in this workbook, it really wasn't until I began journaling in earnest, trying to feel God within the words I was receiving, that I was able to get the full measure of who He was and what He wanted for my life. But the message came through. God's message will always come through. And his message to me at that time is what nurtured the meditations in *Each Day a New Beginning*. I would never have guessed that my struggle to know God was part of His plan for me. Hallelujah.

I have come to believe that God becomes known to each of us in a way He knows will be noticed. How did you first notice God? It's well worth savoring that recollection because there may come a time when you begin to doubt for a spell that He is still there. Remembering how He came will quiet your moment of doubt.

Please share that time when you first noticed His presence here:

_____

_____

_____

_____

_____

_____

_____

_____

And did He have a special message for you? If so, what was that message?

_____

_____

_____

_____

_____

_____

_____

Uncovering the Authentic Self

While considering the way we progress in our lives, even if it's only inch by inch, I've had some thoughts about how we learn more of the truth of ourselves. As I said in *Each Day a New Beginning*: "It's not an easy task to discover who we really are. It's an even harder job to love and accept the person we discover." And I do believe that this can't happen in one fell swoop, but rather incrementally.

When I first got sober, I couldn't have honestly defined who I was to you. I didn't know. I could have said I was working on my doctorate. I could have said I was an alcoholic in recovery, and divorced. And I could have admitted to feeling great anxiety most days. But I didn't know who I was inside—not really.

It took the first few years in AA and Al-Anon too, coupled with my study of *A Course in Miracles,* for me to gather the pieces together of who I was and what made me tick. Little by little, inch by inch, I could see I suffered from codependency, which made me both a caregiver and a seeker of your undivided care. In other words, I was desperate for attention, and it didn't even have to be healthy attention. For years before recovery, in fact, my attention seeking had led me into many dark alleys. Thank goodness God walked with me.

But I now recognize myself as a loving, generally kind woman who is eager to support the healthy efforts of others. I want to feel peaceful and to be a purveyor of peace. I want to encourage, not disparage. I want to rise "above the battleground of conflict" to show there is another way to navigate the circumstances we find ourselves in.

How about you? What do you know about yourself now? How have you changed? What tiny moments in your recent past reveal the person within?

Here and now is the time to share the thoughts that have come to mind:

_____

_____

_____

_____

_____

_____

_____

_____

_____

_____

_____

_____

_____

Learning What Is Yours to Change on the Path to Serenity

Living one moment at a time is of course comparable to moving forward inch by inch. Frankly, our lives can't unfold in any other way. No matter how hard we might want to change this fact, time passes one moment, one inch at a time; and God is present for each one of them—and always will be.

Why would we want to try to change the unchangeable? Accepting what is a fact of our lives is so much more pleasant. And we will not discover the blessing of peace any other way.

Perhaps peace hasn't yet become as important to you as it is to me. Maybe that's one of the things that changes as we age, and I'm no doubt considerably older than many of you reading this passage now. But peace will be sought after in time. I think that's doubtless a fact of one's life as we age. You will get tired of the unnecessary stress of trying to change who and what can't be changed. We all do. But the good news is that nothing has to be changed immediately anyway, and every change in us can be handled incrementally, or in other words, inch by inch. As a matter of fact, most changes can't happen any other way.

The "Serenity Prayer," which is one of the cornerstones of every twelve-step program, offers us another way of looking at how our lives can change and ultimately move forward one moment, one step, and one inch at a time. This prayer so comfortingly helps us to work on what we can change and understand that which isn't ours to change. It establishes so clearly the difference between what is ours to do and what isn't ours. It's life-changing, and it all happens with the passage of time. How convenient, wouldn't you agree?

Your life has changed, no doubt significantly, since being introduced to a recovery path. But I think far too often we roll with the changes, hardly giving them a second glance. One really good exercise is to focus on the changes you have already made, as well as those things you still hope to change. And for good measure, give some careful thought to all of the things you have tried to change that you can now see weren't ever yours to focus on anyway.

Being willing to practice all of the "Serenity Prayer" is the only way to feel the real peace that's promised us one moment at a time. Of course, that also means one inch at a time, as we move forward.

What are those ever so significant changes, even small ones, that are asking to be recounted here? Allow yourself to feel good about each one of them. No change you have needed to make was superfluous to the fuller journey of your life.

No better place than right here and now to share this collection of changes:

_____

_____

_____

_____

_____

_____

_____

_____

Helping Others Helps Us Too

Not only do we need to move ourselves forward little by little, but it behooves us to help others move forward too. And guess what? The people who are traveling with you in this life are the very ones God is quietly suggesting that you offer a bit of help. As I suggested in *Each Day a New Beginning*, "Someone needs a word of encouragement from me. I will brighten her/his vision of the future."

Can you think of a few people you have helped to move forward in the recent past? Maybe no one comes immediately to mind, but I assure you, you have helped many others. Maybe it was a simple gesture of kindness to a total stranger, or a loan of money or a favorite book to a family member. Perhaps you agreed to be a sponsor to a newcomer to our way of life. That gift not only helps him or her but you as well.

And it's not about a big boost of help but a tiny one. What can be accomplished in a moment of your time is really all that's ever expected. Helping that person make a tiny forward movement moves both of you forward, and that's a job well done. Not very complicated, is it?

Take some time now to reflect on the myriad ways you have stepped up to the bat to help someone else. They no doubt number in the hundreds. List a few of them here, and take time to remember how much each gesture helped you too:

_____

_____

_____

_____

_____

_____

_____

_____

_____

_____

Write here after some further reflection:

_____

_____

_____

_____

_____

_____

_____

_____

_____

The Power of Perspective

Where we are right now is the result of the accumulation of millions of tiny steps forward. Even when we think we are standing still, perhaps quietly reflecting or meditating in our easy chair, the moments are slipping by and we are moving forward, perhaps undetectably, but forward nonetheless.

Perhaps this idea is more easily grasped when we consider where we were and what we were doing only twenty-four hours ago—or even just twelve hours ago. It's not likely we had any clear idea of exactly what we would be doing right now, but here we are. Perhaps content; perhaps not. But a shift in our perspective can change everything in this moment.

That's one absolutely thrilling aspect about our lives on this recovery path. We can ask to see "whatever is before us" differently—and a shift will occur in a nanosecond. I have learned it's quite possible to slip from a bad mood into a far more positive mood by making the decision to change my mind. Hopefully you have experienced this too. And if you haven't yet, it's my suggestion that you add this tool to your recovery toolbox immediately.

You and I can see our lives from whatever perspective we select in the blink of an eye. If you find yourself in an uncomfortable position or about to participate in an unnecessary conflict, that's the perfect time to say to the God of your understanding: "Help me see this differently." I can promise, after my years of relying on this tool, that you will feel a palpable sense of relief. You will be freed from the need to say or do anything. You will experience peace in that moment, a peace you can continue to relish for as long as you want, one moment at a time.

Have you missed some opportunities of late to ask your Higher Power to help you see something in a different way? Reflecting on how a situation might have turned out differently may give you the impetus to turn to this tool and apply it in the future. Before moving on, let's think about this tool and how its application could just make all the difference in the level of peace you may come to enjoy every day of your life.

After briefly reviewing your recent past, share what you have discovered about how this tool could have helped you. Describe in detail how some situation that troubled you might have dramatically changed.

Here is the place to share:

_____

_____

_____

_____

_____

_____

_____

_____

_____

_____

_____

Chapter 8

Let's Choose Peace in Our Lives

The idea of choosing to be peaceful rather than fearful, angry, right, or deeply or even mildly upset over any number of large or small situations is an available choice just crying out to be made. However, far too often we allow the peaceful choice to be ignored. Actually, many of us may not even realize peace is a choice. And we need to ask ourselves why.

Why would we rather be living in a state of distress than embraced by the comfort of a peaceful heart? It can only be because we have decided to allow the ego to be in charge of our thinking, and thus of our lives. Fortunately, we can say no to the ego in a nanosecond, and peace waits in the wings to comfort us just as quickly as we open our hearts to it. The question, however, is do we even realize we have the choice to live a peaceful life or not?

I certainly didn't appreciate the power of the peaceful choice for far too many years of my life. Frankly, it never occurred to me that it was a choice. I was way too used to letting my ego pull me from pillar to post. It seems strange now, in fact, to realize I always had the option to change my mind. Peace was simply an elusive state of mind that "just happened," I thought—not a choice. And to me it was surely elusive.

In fact, it wasn't until I added *A Course in Miracles* to my twelve-step recovery in the early '80s that I had any real grasp of how available peace is to a mind that wants it. Prior to that, whatever anyone else said or did usually determined my state of mind. And far too often, "those people" weren't saying or doing what I wanted them to do, so peace wasn't even on my radar screen. When you or I let others define how we feel or what we might next do, the choice to be peaceful isn't a choice at all.

We can change, however. And that's the relevant piece of information here. No one is in charge of your state of mind but you. *A Course in Miracles* says we have two voices in our minds; one is the ego, and it speaks first and is loudest and always wrong! The other voice is our Higher Power, who will always lead us to a peaceful place. Pretty easy choice as to which one you'd rather listen to. Right?

What I'd like to suggest here is that you reflect on some of your recent choices. You surely did choose peace over anger at some point in the recent past. But then there were those times you listened to the ego. We all have those times. Trust me; I'm soon to be eighty-five and forty-eight years sober, and I still have those times. It's about progress, remember?

Have you done enough reflecting now? If so, it's time to write about some choices you made, both good and not so good. You and I need to keep looking inwards if we want to become our better selves.

Here's the place:

_____

_____

_____

_____

_____

Turning the Course of Our Stories Toward Peace

"Each of us tells a story with our lives, one different from all other stories and yet necessary to the telling of many other stories, too." This quote from *Each Day a New Beginning* offers a great backdrop to seeing how our behavior serves to reflect whether we are living with the ego or our Higher Power as our guide. Our interaction with others is the tipoff, in every encounter.

Sometimes we may not choose to listen to the peaceful guidance from our Higher Power. And that's okay. But we will never find peace if the ego has taken control. The people we encounter may well have their peace of mind disrupted too. And unfortunately, the ripple effect goes much further than that sole individual. Whomever we touch with the residue from our unharmonious state of mind may well pass that residue on to multitudes of others as well.

When I stop to consider that what I say or do to you has really far-reaching consequences, it does give me reason to pause. And pausing before we say or do anything can change the experience we are about to have. Is it really a hard choice to pause and ask, "Who do I want in the driver's seat here?" I think not, but the pause is the key. If we want peace—and we'd be foolish not to want peace—all you and I have to do is honor the voice of the Higher Power. He/She will always encourage a peaceful encounter.

You have created a lot of peaceful stories, and likely some which were not so peaceful as well. Now might be a good time to revisit some of those for the purpose of reminding yourself what each kind of story involved. The good news is that you always have the power to make every story one that peacefully embraces not only you but whomever you are encountering too.

When did you most recently contribute to a peaceful story that included someone else? What prompted your contribution? Think a bit and then share that story here:

_____

_____

_____

_____

_____

_____

_____

_____

_____

_____

_____

_____

_____

_____

Rewind the Past

Knowing that our words have the ability to impact multitudes of people over time is an extremely powerful awareness, isn't it? No doubt you have had multiple experiences when you wished you could take something back that you said or did. But as the saying goes, "Even God can't change the past." What was said or done is done—period. But we can make the commitment to ourselves, one day, one moment at a time, to do better. And that's hopeful, I think.

I personally have had many times I wished I could take something back that I'd said. It's usually been to my husband, since he is the person I see on a daily, nearly constant basis. But once out of the mouth, what's done is done. Fortunately, you and I have learned with the help of the program we share that making an amend is always accessible to us. And being at odds with others generally has far-reaching consequences. What I say to you, when it isn't kind, not only impacts our relationship but can also send both of us into other relationships, carrying with us less than loving feelings from the previous interaction.

How lucky for us that we can stop the momentum of this tailspin just as quickly as it began. And we stop it by employing the proverbial pause, and seeking in each moment the loving comfort and guidance of our Higher Power. He/She has never left our side, and never will, in fact. If we want to do better, we have the solution at our disposal. All we have to do is apply it.

Have you had times in your recent past that you missed an opportunity to do better? Can you see now what would have been a better action, response, or even quiet thought? As already mentioned, we can't undo the past, but we can use it as the launching pad to make for a better present.

Take some time to recall what you said or did, and then consider what might have been a better choice. Writing about that episode will be helpful in your work to retrain your thinking.

When you are ready to write, go for it here:

_____

_____

_____

_____

_____

_____

_____

_____

_____

_____

_____

Walk the Path of Peace

"Give Peace a Chance" was a song written by John Lennon decades ago, one that will always ring true. Even though he was referring to the Vietnam War at the time, it matters not. Hopefully the idea still resonates.

If we did live our lives more peacefully, we could be making a valuable difference on the world stage with every breath we take. It may not seem like our tiny actions could matter, but that's not true. Every action we take matters. That was always true, and it will always be true.

Today is a great day to give peace a chance. If you make the decision upon arising to live each moment peacefully that day, it just might surprise you how much your life will change.

Just for today, one moment at a time, relish the possibility of a peaceful state of mind. You are the one in charge. You have always been in charge, and this is one fact that will never change. Now, it's true that you have the guiding hand of God to help you maintain a peaceful demeanor. All that's required of you is a little willingness to allow Him to nudge you in the right direction, and then to say the right words and think the right thoughts that precede every right, peaceful encounter.

Life really doesn't have to be as tumultuous as you and I make it. We simply let the ego decide for us how to behave, and then all hell tends to break loose. Life is just too short to live in the maelstrom of the ego's dictates. I can assure you, at eighty-five, that making the choice to "*see peace instead of this*" is the far wiser and certainly gentler path on which to journey.

The question for you right now is this: Are you walking the gentle peaceful path? And if not, what is tripping you up? You are in charge—you and God, that is.

It's time for reflection and writing; focus on the path you are walking and why you think that is your path so far. And if you'd like to tweak it a bit, just what would you do?

Here is the place:

_____

_____

_____

_____

_____

_____

_____

_____

_____

_____

_____

_____

Peace Is Within Our Reach

"No circumstance demands suffering. Every circumstance has a silver lining. In one instance you may choose to feel self-pity; in the next gladness." This quote from *Each Day a New Beginning* is a good reminder that no one can decide for us how we are going to interpret the experiences of our lives.

The very same set of circumstances may strike one person one way while you may see those circumstances in a far different way. That's the power of the mind. And that's why making the decision to "see peace instead of this," whatever *this* may be, is not only a possibility but a wise choice.

Hopefully you realize, as I have come to realize, that we don't ever have to be stuck in a state of mind that isn't peaceful. Does that mean that we will always choose to be at peace? I certainly can't claim that I'm always living there. But I do know it's only a change of mind away. I hope you can see the same is true for you.

But perhaps the even bigger idea to consider here is why "seeing peace instead of this" is so important. To me, it's important because the alternative to peace is not only unpleasant but provokes great anxiety in me. Your response may not be like mine at all, but you and I both know how peace feels to us. And I'm guessing it's a feeling you'd prefer to entertain rather than whatever its opposite might be.

I grew up in a household that seldom felt peaceful. Perhaps that's where my aversion to the state of anxiety comes from. I simply know that life is too short, particularly for me as I've aged, to waste many moments anywhere but in the bosom of peace. Regardless of your age, I'm thinking you might share this opinion. And let's not forget that when we aren't at peace, we are interacting with others in a way that might interfere with their peace of mind as well.

Consider when you last felt the blessing of a peaceful heart. Can you remember what initiated it? Can you recapture that state of mind? It is possible, you know. You are the one in charge.

Share your thoughts about the above questions here:

_____

_____

_____

_____

_____

_____

_____

_____

_____

_____

_____

_____

Strengthening a Centered Sense of Being

I still remember as though it were yesterday reading *Why Am I Afraid to Tell You Who I Am?* by John Powell. I think it's worth returning to this book because of the lesson it offered me.

I was using it as a text in a personal writing class I was teaching at the University of Minnesota in 1971. As you might recall, Powell's friend, a journalist, had been treated very rudely by a newspaper vendor as they strolled the New York city streets. However, his friend was extremely kind regardless. Powell asked him why he was so nice to the disrespectful individual. His friend replied, "Why should I let him decide what kind of a day I'm going to have?"

I was stunned. I had let others decide how I was going to feel for years—a classic case of codependency. And it really didn't matter who you were; if you brushed me off or spoke unkindly to me, I was sure the fault was mine. Al-Anon taught me so much about the malady of codependency. Being able to detach from others' words and actions truly allows us to live our own lives.

Perhaps how others treated you was never a problem. If not, how fortunate for you. But it might be a good exercise anyway to look at your past, if only briefly, to see how you handled the words and actions of others. You have a great chance to show others the way if you have lived comfortably unaffected by the behavior of others. And if you, like me, were affected, how did you begin the transformation of your life?

Think carefully about how you have navigated your journey. Were you able to allow others their put-downs, knowing they didn't really define you? That's a sign of real emotional health when we can walk anywhere among others, knowing full well who we are and who we are not. No one else ever has to be in charge of any feeling you have—not ever. Peace can be your constant companion.

Can you recall times when you let someone else define you or control how you felt? (Or when someone else at least tried to do that, if you managed to escape their attempts?) It happens all of the time. And you and I can be the culprits too; we can try to control the feelings of others. Backing away from any attempt to do so is an available choice. Think a bit on both of these scenarios: being controlled, or trying to control another. Then prepare yourself to write about how either of these situations can or did affect you.

Are you ready to write? Consider sharing an example or two here of times when you have let someone else "steal" your peace of mind, or other scenarios involving these interpersonal dynamics:

_____

_____

_____

_____

_____

_____

_____

_____

Now take a moment to make a plan about what you might do in the face of this kind of disruption in the future.

Please share that plan here:

_____

_____

_____

_____

_____

_____

_____

_____

_____

_____

_____

Being in charge of ourselves is so healthy. And being willing to let others do the same frees all of us.

Returning Our Awareness to Where We Are

"All that matters passes before us now, at this moment." This quote from *Each Day a New Beginning* rather stops me in my tracks. The emphasis on this moment we have focused on before, assuredly. But even by so few words we are brought to attention, aren't we?

What the quote says is that this very moment, along with the people we encounter right here and now, is clearly all that matters. The simplicity of the statement is undeniable, but the meaning encompassed within it is daunting. Forget all else, it says. Pay heed only to the here and now.

We have to stop wherever we are and consider where our mind is. Mine has not been very peaceful lately, not in any moment. Let me share my story:

I have been going through a spell of unusual computer issues. I haven't been able to start or get into video meetings on my computer lately. This might not be a big issue for many, but I teach a couple of classes via Zoom and host a few meetings that way as well. Without going into the granular details, having this experience has left me doubting myself in many other realms too, which has had even more of an impact on my days than the technical problem itself.

I have at times allowed my fear to block out the awareness of the constant presence of my Higher Power. I am very aware that He is still within, but I have felt far removed from Him. And that's a place I need not go. I don't know if you ever fall into the trap of fear, but if you do, it's because you, too, have simply forgotten Who is here, now, and will always be present.

If you have gone through a situation that overwhelmed you of late, this might be a good place and time to share it so that you can look at it with some objectivity. Remember, God is on hand to look at it with you.

Reflect and then share here:

_____

_____

_____

_____

_____

_____

_____

_____

_____

_____

_____

_____

_____

_____

_____

_____

_____

_____

_____

Times That Test Us

Choosing to see something differently so we can be at peace, rather than filled with the anxiety that can sometimes overwhelm us, is such a gentle and available choice. And it can be our default position if only we decide that we are worthy of being at peace all of the time. It truly is the most reasonable choice. And it impacts all of those other people we come into contact with too. Myriad individuals are blessed every time we make this simple choice.

I am a work in progress! In some respects, we all are. But my recent struggles with computer issues have resulted in my failing to rely on all of the truths I so often write and speak about; for instance, the awareness that everything is always in right order because God is my constant companion. How can I so easily dismiss this when it would ease my mind and heart to rely on this understanding?

In the meantime, I have many anxious moments, and they interfere with everything else in my life. At this juncture of my life, I'm simply not living in the calm, peaceful bosom of my Companion. I know full well He/She hasn't deserted me. I'm the one missing in action.

I surely hope you don't find yourself in my predicament very often, but it isn't all that unusual to slip into these crevasses. They are part of the journey, after all. And they are meant to remind us of the need to never forget to turn to the God of our understanding for help and peace of mind. God's presence simply cannot desert us. It lives at our very core. How lucky you and I are that this is a fact of our lives that will never change. Never ever.

Do you ever find yourself floundering because you have forgotten the constancy of God? Does your trust in His/Her presence ever wane? In those moments or spans of time, what do you see as your solution? Having one is the quickest way to get yourself back on track. It's time now to reflect on your solution strategy; and if you don't have one readily available, might it be time to develop one?

Take some time to think about this and then recount for yourself just what you have done or would do if you were faced with the kind of dilemma I outlined. Being overwhelmed by anxiety is never necessary, but having a go-to plan to recenter yourself when it strikes offers the kind of relief we deserve. Remember, we can always "see peace instead of this."

Share your thoughts here:

_____

_____

_____

_____

_____

_____

_____

_____

_____

_____

Freeing the Heart to Love and Choose Peace

To quote *Each Day a New Beginning*, "I am charged with only one responsibility today: to love someone dearly and wholly." Is this a difficult assignment? I think not. But we can make it harder by allowing our ego to dictate our assumptions about others.

The ego never wants us to love anyone. As a matter of fact, it's always pushing us to judge or attack others. And if we let it define us in all of the encounters heading our way today, we will not experience the peace we deserve, even though peace is always only a simple decision away.

I know that peace of mind calls to me. And I'm pretty convinced that it sits on your doorstep too. Why do we not embrace it more consistently? Being at peace is so freeing. Why do you and I choose otherwise so often? Actually, I'm not really convinced we consciously do choose otherwise. I think we fall into the trap of the sneaky ego that sits waiting for us to lose sight of who we really want to be.

Take a moment here to think about who you really want to be. Is that how you show up in most instances of your life? Or are you allowing the ego to take you hostage before you even realize what has happened? We need not feel ashamed if that's what so often happens to us. Generally it's an unconscious choice. You and I simply need to recognize that this is the case, and then make another choice. How hard is that?

If you feel like the ego is stealing your peace of mind, how might you counter that situation today? Remember, it's nearly impossible to focus on loving anyone else if the ego has taken charge of your thinking. And your only responsibility today is to love at least one other person completely. How do you intend to confront this situation if it is standing in your way today or has been hindering you sometime in this last week? You need a plan of action. And there is no better time than now to devise it.

What can I do if loving others isn't coming easily?

_____

_____

_____

_____

_____

_____

_____

_____

_____

_____

_____

_____

Chapter 9

....

Our Timeline Informs Us of Who We Were and Who We May Become

Hindsight is a valuable tool. It reveals where we were, most assuredly, but also highlights the connections between the myriad occurrences in our past. These connections can serve as potential indicators of where our journey may be taking us next. There are always connections.

For instance, when I revisit the experiences I had in my first marriage and how it ended, and then reflect carefully on the next leg of my journey, which was to enter graduate school, where I earned a doctorate, I can see how the closing of one door was the precursor to the opening of a door I had never fathomed I would be walking through.

The same was true much earlier in my life as well. My first drink at age thirteen set the stage for the forty-eight years in recovery from alcoholism that I now enjoy, one day at a time. But I could never have imagined the glory days ahead at thirteen. Of course, they were slow in coming. But they came. Why would I expect this kind of unfolding to change as I look to the next stage of my life? Indeed, I don't.

In my eighth decade, I'm definitely not sure what lies ahead. But I do know that whatever it is, it will follow quite perfectly on the heels of whatever has preceded it. That's simply how our lives unfold: Perfectly. While it's true they may not feel smooth and perfect during the unfolding, you and I can count on the active involvement of God in how everything comes to pass. There is simply no other way for our lives to move forward. God will be present. After all, God is the conductor of the orchestra we are sitting in.

My guess is that you may have little or no idea about what lies ahead either. Perhaps there is a new job in your future or a move to a new location. Our relationships are seldom static, so some may end or otherwise transform and be replaced by new ones. The one thing you and I can count on is the constant presence of God as we walk through whatever the changes are. And don't forget what I pointed out in an earlier chapter; we have always been prepared for whatever change comes along. We simply might not recognize it initially. Nothing comes unbidden, and we will be grateful for the growth in due time.

Take some time now to glance back at your timeline. If you have never drawn one, now would be a very good time to draw one. Each one of us needs to honor who we have been, in light of where we have been and any connections between the events that seem to stand out. Whatever gets your attention is actually worth far more than a glance too. It's calling to you. Nothing that ever happened should be overlooked. Every moment of our lives has been spirit filled.

Throughout this chapter you will be directed to pay heed to your timeline; so for this initial exercise, please focus only on the first decade of your life. My first decade still calls me to attention. I think yours may do so as well. In myriad ways it left its imprint on your remaining life, so don't consider anything from your early life that invites your attention as unimportant.

You may need to daydream a bit to bring forth the kind of recollections you need to fulfill this exercise. Take all the time you need. There is no hurry. Your life, past, present, and whatever the future might hold is all that matters right now.

What is calling to you when you turn your attention to your first decade? Please share here whatever you know wants to be looked at more clearly now with the gift of hindsight:

_____

_____

_____

_____

_____

_____

_____

_____

_____

_____

_____

_____

Did you discover some recollections that you really didn't want to focus on? Share them anyway. They may help you to better understand something that occasionally trips you up even these many years later:

_____

_____

_____

_____

_____

_____

_____

_____

_____

_____

_____

_____

Remembering Our Successes

One major point of a timeline is to measure our successes. We have had many. We may not have considered them very big deals at the time, but they contributed in necessary ways to where our journey was designed to take us next, step by step, experience by experience, moment by moment. There was always a significant explanation for every step forward and every detour too. Nothing appeared on our radar screen by accident—nothing at all.

One of my successes was becoming an author, certainly not a career I had set my sights on before the opportunity presented itself. And as I have pointed out in earlier sections, I hit many stumbling blocks on my way to this career. My alcoholism could easily have derailed me; and yet it was a primary contributing factor to what God had been planning for me all along.

Perhaps it sounds strange to you when I say that God was part of the earlier, very troubling journey I was stumbling through, but I do believe that. God was always very present. God always had a destination in mind, and I am now enjoying the fruits of that destination as I write each one of these words.

Frankly, I think the same is true for you too. Wherever you are right now and wherever your timeline reveals that you were last year or five years ago, it was never an accident. You were where you needed to be, and whatever successes you were enjoying, even the relatively small ones were calling your name.

Let's take some time right now for you to pay homage to some of the successes on your timeline. Surely there have been many. Some might have seemed tiny at the time, but they too played a role in a future success. Every incident in our lives is perfect, happening in its right time and our right time too. God was always the One in charge—*always*.

Take some time right now to reflect on some of the successes in your past. Fond memories are good for our souls. After you have meditated a time about this, please share a few of those memorable successes so you can relive them and feed your soul:

_____

_____

_____

_____

_____

_____

_____

_____

_____

_____

_____

_____

_____

_____

_____

_____

Even Our Youthful Mishaps Served to Bring Us Here

Your teenage years may well have been both exciting and troubling. Mine certainly were. My drinking had not become a daily habit yet, but I had bouts of drinking at the wrong time and in the wrong places. Your timeline might not be like mine at all but let me share a bit. My sharing might trigger some recalls for you. After all, it's quite possible that we aren't so very different.

At my suggestion, my best girlfriend and I snuck beer into high school and openly drank it standing before a raised window on the second floor of the school, waving to all of our friends. That we weren't thrown out of school was simply because we were "in the right crowd."

It's not a memory I'm proud of, but it was a strong indicator of the path I was on. In college, I was put on social probation because of drinking openly on the sidewalk while walking to a college class and being in a fraternity after hours. And I laughed about both incidents, seeing neither one of them as serious or troubling in any way.

I review them now as definite signs of where I was headed. But was my destination ultimately bad? No. And yet, I might well have slipped off the rails completely. That I didn't was due to one thing. And you know what that one thing was.

I know you didn't completely slip off the rails either, or you wouldn't be reading this workbook now. But did you have some experiences in your teens like mine, ones that were pointing in a direction you maybe hadn't counted on going? Can you make better sense of them now? Do you see how they might have been one of the necessary links in the timeline? It might not be completely clear when you first ponder it, but look again, perhaps with greater attention this second time. Every link mattered. Every experience mattered—even the ones that were hardly memorable at all.

What comes to mind right now as a memory, good or bad, that you now know was signaling where you were heading, at least for a while? When you feel like writing about the memory, go for it:

_____

_____

_____

_____

_____

_____

_____

_____

_____

_____

Charting Past Milestones

Our first real job was significant for most of us. Seldom did it point to what we were going to be doing for the rest of our lives, but it did often indicate some key characteristics about us. Let's delve into this category next. Out timeline offers us the information we need.

Although I did actually begin working at age twelve at the community park in Lafayette, Indiana, selling tickets on a "kiddie ride," it was significant in only one way: I took it seriously. And I felt good about earning my own money.

But I landed my first real job while I was in high school. I worked in a department store after school and on weekends. It was a very responsible job, and I was being groomed by my boss to go into merchandizing at Purdue. Even though I didn't end up pursuing that goal, I was looked up to and considered extremely competent. I felt proud because I had sought that job when I was only fifteen. My only other option was to work at my uncle's grocery store, and that was not very appealing.

Working "downtown" made me feel very grown-up. I got a discount on all of my clothes too. I look back at the memory with some pride as a time when I dared to do what my sisters had not had the courage to do. I felt it prepared me for better things ahead. It surely was no straight line from there to graduate school more than fifteen years later, but any act of courage does inspire us to try other acts requiring equal or greater courage. Much in my life reflects myriad times when I dared to go that extra step.

I'm guessing you can see the connecting dots in how some of your earlier pursuits too were linked with experiences, perhaps even challenges, that paid a visit later in your life. I do think it's important to remember that you and I have been prepared for every situation that comes calling. Of course, that doesn't mean we will recognize how our previous experiences led us to the crossroads we are now facing, but trust me; you were prepared. And you can make the most of any experience. In fact, up until now, you have managed to integrate whatever each experience had to offer. That's how you got to where you are right now. Bravo for you. And the rest is yet to come.

Let's take some time here to reflect once again on some of the connecting dots on the timeline. If you haven't done this before, be prepared to be pleasantly surprised. It's no accident where you find yourself now—no accident at all.

Reflect, appreciate, and then share what comes to you:

_____

_____

_____

_____

_____

_____

_____

_____

_____

_____

Taking Another Look at Past Challenges

"We must stretch to become all we are meant to be." This quote from *Each Day a New Beginning* has been a guiding force for many of us our entire lives. Perhaps in our addictions we failed to go that extra mile, but we are blessed to have the chance to "do over" much that we failed to do to our liking in the past.

And when we review our timeline, we can see ever so clearly all of those times we simply took a ride rather than drive our bus. But we need not fret. We did the best we could at that time. And now we are living with a new perspective that helps us to seize each moment with greater understanding.

I am so grateful to be living with the belief that there is no need for shame or self-recrimination. And like you, I have learned this from the tools of the Twelve Steps. Recovery has taught me so much. I'm sure you can also count innumerable ways in which you have learned to see your life, both the past and the present, differently. And assuredly that means we will be able to see our opportunities differently in the future too, and more clearly.

To reiterate an idea that I have shared earlier, in this book and in other books too: If an opportunity to experience something pays a visit when we feel unready for it, we can let it pass us by for now. What we need to learn will revisit us until the time when we say, "Now." That's a really significant truth we can count on. Any lesson we need to fulfill the purpose for which we were born won't pass us by permanently. Each one of us is absolutely necessary to the unfolding of every one of us—if not now, at some future time. And that's truly great news. You are necessary, as am I.

It's a great exercise to look at one's timeline and take notice of all the times it's now apparent that you were necessary to what was happening in the circle of people you had been called to join. You "seized the moment." Most likely you often paid no heed at all to many of these situations you were a part of. I surely lived "unconsciously" for decades of my life. For sure I was aware when I felt slighted, or worse, rejected; but lots of my life was spent just going along with whatever seemed to be next in line for my attention.

Standing back now, as I'm suggesting you do, and looking at a certain period of your life might be extremely revealing. What in your past snuck by you at the time it first happened? Do you see the mark it actually made on what followed? How do you think noticing that experience now, as though for the first time, might impact your future timeline? Remember, nothing that happens to us is isolated from everything else that happens to us. Our lives are a composite of all of their events—all of them; and of all the people we encounter along the way.

What from your timeline is waving to get your attention right now? Is it something that you can see did stretch you? Or is it something that might have but you passed it by? The important thing here is to look, and look closely at where you were at specific times and who sought out your help. He or she needed connection. Were you able to show up? Our showing up is what stretches us and others.

Take time to reflect on what you can now see. What do you feel good about? What might you do differently the next time?

_____

_____

_____

_____

No Chance Meetings

When you look at your timeline, what do you consider your most significant decade, or perhaps span of decades? The length of this significant time period isn't important. The point is that we have had many growth spurts along the way, and some of them came as the result of exciting, though perhaps unexpected, opportunities. Some came because of major stumbles, or worse, tragedies. What's important to honor is that whatever happened and however it presented itself was perfect. Let's never forget, "Nothing happens in God's world by accident."

I must admit that when I first heard this statement and then read it in the Big Book of Alcoholics Anonymous, I was more than a little skeptical. There were way too many things on the world stage that didn't seem to jibe with this statement. And even in my own life, how could these untold numbers of difficult things be part of God's bigger plan? Experiencing sexual abuse as a young girl? Alcoholic behavior beginning at age thirteen? An unwanted divorce at age thirty-two?

What I had to come to terms with was that I didn't necessarily have to understand the truth for it to be true. It was about acceptance. And the Big Book also had a significant quote about acceptance. It is the answer to all of my problems!

Both of these ideas are treasured by most of us walking the recovery path. And it's quite likely that most of us felt some doubt about their validity when first introduced to them. But something changed, at least for me. I wanted to live a more peaceful life. And one sure way to grasp more peace is to say *all is well*—and mean it!

Relying on hindsight is such a gift to me. And hopefully it is for you too. It honestly does show us the whys and the hows of our journey. If we take note of how one experience intersected with another, specifically noticing the situations both before and following the intersection, we will be apprised of the role God was playing in our lives. God was always present. And we didn't need to understand this or even believe it to make it true.

Did that mean God caused the awful things that might have happened? I don't think so, but He was there to walk us through the lessons we had the opportunity to grasp from the experiences, lessons that were indeed necessary for us to complete the journey we are here to make.

I find it pretty awesome to absorb how quietly God comes into the picture to set things right. After all, we do need to end up where we have been called to be; if not now, at another significant intersection. It will happen—it has to happen. And we don't really even have to do a thing to make this true. Taking note of how smoothly all of this unfolds is what can offer us the comfort we need when we are unsure about what to do next. We will always know. The answer is to listen. The guidance will come. It did come, in fact—again and again. Our timeline shows that.

Now it's time for you to look once again at your timeline. Can you see how God ushered you toward some significant intersections? What were those intersections, and what did you ultimately learn from them? Remember, not all intersections seemed pleasing at the time, but they did offer you a lesson you came to understand later.

Share what you have learned from this visit to your timeline:

_____

_____

_____

_____

_____

_____

_____

_____

_____

_____

_____

_____

_____

_____

_____

_____

_____

_____

_____

_____

_____

Beyond Random Encounters

Our relationships have so much to teach us. In fact, they are the very reason we are here. We were scheduled to experience each one of them before we even came into this existence, according to spiritual intuitive author Caroline Myss. And that idea surely has become a foundation of my personal philosophy. It explains so much, and it also relieves me of worry about any future encounters too. They will come when their time is right.

Does this mean we love all our encounters? Certainly not. Some we may abhor, in fact. Some may frighten us and push us into making thoughtless decisions. Others may encourage us to entertain ideas that are not for our ultimate good. But all relationships, no matter how long they last or if they are merely fleeting, come as bidden. Hindsight can offer us a way to understand them. That's one way having a timeline can be helpful. It's all about the connections.

Over the years I have seen so many connections to the events in my life, connections that I never noticed when they were happening. And I don't think that's unusual. In the midst of a situation, we very seldom have the impetus to see how it might be following quite smoothly on the heels of what preceded it. But it did. And it always will. In fact, any number of "situations" will turn out to be quite cozily interconnected—and rightly so. Let's not forget, our lives have been orchestrated and the Conductor is always present.

For certain I didn't see how the events that transpired as my life seemed to be falling apart were actually introducing me to one of the most significant, challenging, and successful endeavors I could ever have imagined. We don't see what is on the radar screen for our future. But it's there, and it will capture not only our attention but our studied involvement when the time is right. How lucky we are that the plans for our lives have been so concretely laid out. It matters not at all that we may be the last to know. We will do our part on cue.

You have been doing your part for many years. No doubt, like me, you didn't realize exactly why that part was yours, but it called to you, and you answered. The sweet news is that you will always answer; if not the first time the call comes, then at another even more perfect time. I think scoping your timeline will highlight this for you. Take some time now to do this, and when you feel ready, share here what you discover about a few of the many connections, what they were, and what you gained by them.

Reflect and then write here:

_____

_____

_____

_____

_____

_____

_____

_____

_____

From Past Tapestries to Future Threads

Perhaps you are thinking, "What's the point of a timeline? Do I really care about all of life's events being laid out in such an orderly fashion?" I think with the advancement of years, we can see its value better. In the midst of our lives, certainly in the midst of any one experience, we seldom see the strategic role it is actually playing, the way it is snuggling up to the event that preceded it.

But assuredly, every stop along the way has had its purpose. And what preceded each stop might well be seen as the "door opener" to something extremely significant.

Let's just accept the fact that every experience we have ever had was significant and we didn't have to see its importance at the time. In retrospect, we can now see the myriad threads of this tapestry our lives have been weaving from the day of our birth until now. To reiterate, each thread has been absolutely necessary for the pattern of our lives to emerge.

Personally, I have loved reviewing my timeline. Additionally, the fact that our lives are still in the process of weaving a tapestry unique to ourselves fills my heart with gladness and my mind with colorful imagery. I certainly lived through some dark times, but they were offset by achievements I had never anticipated I would garner. My guess is that's been true for you too. Dark times are to be expected on occasion as we navigate the journey that has been perfectly our own. But the highlights were just as expected. And no doubt, they visited us pretty equally.

What's extremely important in this review, however, is that we do not overlook any experience based on the assumption that it wasn't important enough to acknowledge. Indeed, every single point on the timeline not only was important but remains so. Let's not forget, our lives are still unfolding.

Once again we have come to the time for you to review the dark times as well as the highlights of your life. We don't always want to revisit the former, but they do have a lot to teach us. Please always remember that you made each and every contract with the specific individual in all the encounters you have had—and those yet to come—before arriving here. There have been no surprises. You simply forgot what you had agreed to learn.

You have learned so many things on this journey so far. You need not list them all at this time, but list a few of them and then be glad for your good fortune. Even those lessons that seemed hard carried you to and through a doorway to the growth you were ready for.

Reflect, meditate, or just sit quietly and let the memories flow. Then begin to share some of the things you have learned:

_____

_____

_____

_____

_____

_____

_____

_____

Let the Pattern of the Past Illuminate the Future

"I will appreciate the design of my life." This quote from *Each Day a New Beginning* fits quite comfortably into our review of our timeline because it quite clearly points to the divine design God had in mind for us.

Have we stumbled on occasion? For sure we have, but those stumbles often clarified a slight detour that was necessary for us to get to our next destination. Simply never doubt that God always had you on His radar screen. As I've repeatedly said throughout this workbook, we are one with God always. There is no other way to be.

As I review the design of my life, particularly these many decades of recovery from addictions coupled with my profession as a writer, I really don't see any change of direction in my future. (Now, it's possible God has a plan that hasn't been revealed yet.) But writing feeds my soul and has done so ever since I discovered the joy of expressing myself through the written word back in my early thirties when I was in graduate school.

Of course, I didn't know then the kind of writing that I'd be doing in time. I was deep into my alcoholism in my early thirties. But writing still brought me solace. And I could sense that I had a "helper" for every word I wrote. Words simply seemed to flow with little or no thought on my part. I just didn't understand who that helper was, but He has remained by my side ever since.

Let's stop to consider the fact, the undeniable fact, that each one of us has had a "helper" for every step of our journey. At times we ignored the helper and took detours that led us astray for a time, but guess what? We got back to where we needed to be. And that will be a fact of our lives from this moment forward.

I don't know if you are able to ascertain from the journey you have completed so far where you might be heading next, but it's a good time to ponder this. Are you content with where you are right now? Or are you itching for some new adventures? Perhaps you are feeling both of these things, contentment but also a sense of kind of looking over the horizon. If you take a careful look at the multitude of experiences you've had up to now and assess just how fulfilling each one was for you, that may well indicate a shift in where you want your journey to take you next.

There is no shame in wanting to stay exactly where you are, doing what you are presently doing. If God has another plan for you, you will be alerted to it. After all, I've already said I'm content to stay put doing what I love so much. You and I get to choose, as we all do, and that's the real beauty of our lives. We are in charge of this choice. So take some time to think about it.

Do you need to come to any decision now about any change of direction? Assuredly not. Just ponder. That's all. Take all the time you need to consider how content you are and even whether a change appeals to you.

Here is where you can pour out your thoughts:

_____

_____

_____

_____

_____

_____

Seeds of Becoming

Which events stand out as the most significant in this last decade of your life? Let's take some time to thoroughly enjoy revisiting these experiences. For most of us they have come after many years of trudging this road to happy destiny. Admittedly, there were rough crevices and boulders that tripped some of us up, but here we are today. We have survived. And we are ready to move forward for however many years we have left.

How and where our forward movement may take us is the question on the minds of many of us. Do we want to repeat some of our earlier experiences because they brought us great joy? That's certainly a choice we can make. Or do we want to dare to try what in earlier years we might have considered unfathomable? That's a choice we can make too.

For many of us, our earlier years were troubled by insecurities. I surely didn't feel that I could even attempt some of the things that I eventually succeeded at doing. In actuality, alcohol gave me the courage to dare to try what had seemed unimaginable.

I surely don't want to sing the praises of alcohol. Indeed not. I have forty-eight years of sobriety in Alcoholics Anonymous. But I was certainly not headed toward graduate school as an undergraduate at Purdue. And I truly don't think I would or could have attempted it at all if I had not found unexpected courage to try the unthinkable that I received from alcohol. But I'm not naive enough to think that alcohol would have continued to take me to the places that God was calling me to be. I was well aware that I had reached the end of the line; that to carry on and finish writing my dissertation, Jack Daniels and I had to part ways.

And now, after completing a PhD and thirty-one books, and after hundreds of workshops and contact with literally millions of readers, I am doing what I know God wants me to do. What might he have planned for my future?

I don't know. And of course, that's true for you as well. But you and I can be certain that the next leg of the journey will be as educational as all of the previous legs.

We are always being led. We are always being "tutored," and we are always meeting the teachers for the lessons we have agreed to learn on this sojourn. They will find us. They have to because we have something to teach them as well.

Who might these next teachers be? Just maybe your last decade has some clues to offer you. Look carefully at your experiences during that time and see if something stands out. Were you ever on the threshold of a new direction? Were you rethinking giving a former experience, a job perhaps, a second try, or even revisiting an old relationship for a second chance? Or were you considering making a big move to a new city, or taking up a new profession or a new way of living your life? There are so many directions that might have called to you, or that are possibly "redialing" you now. Just be aware that whatever calls is calling for a reason. Pay it heed.

I think now is a good time to kick back and let the memories flow. They are full of good information. Sort through them and pick out what speaks loudest to you right now. It's quite possibly the direction to go, at least for the present.

What has this exercise shown you? Share your thoughts here:

_____

_____

_____

_____

_____

Chapter 10

Now Is Our Time

Now is always our time, of course, but what we might consider doing with this specific "now" will vary based on how we may feel at this particular present moment. Our journey, with all its stopping off points, including points you have reviewed throughout these workbook exercises, has brought us to this moment in time; and although we may have felt undirected, that's never been the case.

We have always been directed, but we may not have been all that cognizant of the "director." However, I think through reviewing our timeline, we might now see how very perfectly past experiences did indeed open the doors to those that came after them. There were no extraneous encounters nor any unintended visitors on our paths at any point. Who came and went and what we learned from one another gave meaning to the whole of what had gone before. And will this change as we move forward? I surely think not.

How reassuring it is, at least to me, that there was a director, a companion of sorts, who not only cared about the journey but was very much a part of every step of it. And we can count on that being an unchanged fact for all the nows that lie before us. Does this quiet any anxiety you may feel for the many moments yet to come? I hope so. The past has informed us. Let's allow it to comfort us in any way needed for the unfolding of our future.

Had I known what lay in store for me as I was traipsing through all my wild and crazy alcoholic years, perhaps I'd have sought recovery sooner. But just as quickly as I write that thought, I know that an earlier recovery was not on my trajectory. I got sober at the right time and in the right way in order to meet those individuals whom I had "agreed" to meet at their appointed time. What a stunning realization that is every time I'm reminded of it. I agreed to meet the many men and women, quite a number of whom I no longer can even call by name, because we needed to have our shared "now."

The "now" I am experiencing at this moment is the joy of writing this very book that you, the reader, are now holding in your hands. And this book would not have ever been presented as an idea if my first book, *Each Day a New Beginning,* written more than forty years ago, had not celebrated its anniversary. The one had to precede the other. And so goes life. There is an order to all that is happening—a quite perfect order.

Is there anything in particular that you are anticipating happening in the next few "nows" of your life? Has anything you have recently experienced given you a subtle clue as to where you might be called to go next? Perhaps your path will lead you to an entirely new kind of experience or even a new collection of friends. Might you be embarking on a new hobby that will add a flourish to your life that before now had been missing?

Collecting your thoughts about the recent nows in your life might give you a clue about where you are headed. And then, they might not. But you may well have some unmet dreams about endeavors that interest you that you can explore. The present is all you have. You can, with God's help, make a right turn or keep moving straight ahead. What are you thinking regarding these options? Maybe it's time to meditate a bit. It's your life, after all—yours and God's.

Sharing your thoughts will help you to clarify your dreams and aspirations. They aren't a surprise to God, remember.

Go for it:

_____

_____

_____

_____

_____

_____

_____

_____

_____

_____

_____

_____

_____

_____

_____

_____

_____

Embracing the Present

Letting go of every moment but the one we are currently living is truly the way to peace of mind. We explored peace of mind in an earlier chapter, but there might not be any more important gift that Now brings us than this. Living in the future or lamenting the past is far too common for so many of us. But releasing all else but right now is the only way to find the real purpose for which we have been born. And every one of us does have a purpose quite specific to us. After all, we do know that each individual is unique, unlike everyone else. So of course, our purpose has to be unique as well.

Does that mean we always understand that purpose? Probably not; however, the timeline we reviewed in the last chapter may well have clarified what that purpose was for some. Do we need to know with absolute certainty what our purpose is? I used to think so. But no more. All that's needed is willingness to make each "now" count.

When I came into the rooms of AA and was introduced to the idea of God's will, I was uneasy because I didn't know how to realize the presence of God in the moment, so of course I didn't know how to determine what His will for me was. I can still remember quite vividly the discomfort I felt, a discomfort that I didn't sense others feeling. It never occurred to me that God simply wanted me to be present and kind in the moment to all of the other people with whom I was journeying. That understanding was slow in coming. Didn't God want me to go to Africa or something? Or at least move to one coast or the other?

But finally, though not very quickly, I did get the message about God's will. And I was helped to understand the message by a line in *A Course in Miracles*: "I am here only to be truly helpful..."

Even though that initially didn't feel very specific and certainly not especially grand, in time I was gently eased by the simplicity of the message. It wasn't about doing grand and glorious things; kindness was quite good enough. Just as Mother Teresa was known to have said, "Be kind to everyone, and start with the person standing next to you."

That's the avenue to helpfulness. And it's an assignment I can manage to handle in every now that I have the good fortune to experience. Because I have reached my mid-eighties, I am all too aware that I have far fewer nows remaining than the ones I have already lived. But we all get our allotment. The question to consider is this: Have I made good use of the tens of millions of "nows" I have been given so far? If we find we are doubtful at all about the answer, there is still time to make all that remain a blessing to ourselves and to all who are touched by our interaction in each moment.

What does claiming the most from each "now" mean to you? Are you comfortable sticking with this present moment only? Or do you find yourself looking at the past and wishing you had done or said something different? Or are you, like so many unfortunately, troubled by worry about what's coming around the corner? If you find yourself sucked into either of these projections, you really are missing *life* entirely. Life is Now—and nowhere else. What was is gone forever. And there is no future moment at all. You will arrive at the next "now" only after this one has been lived in full.

What does this topic of Now mean to you? Does it speak to you in a comforting way? Do you see any avenues to making it more meaningful? In what way do you think you might need to change your thinking to get the most from Now? Can you see earlier "nows" that were missed entirely? What was the net loss? There is still plenty of time to change how we navigate what remains of our lives. You don't know how many "nows" you have. But you can make a plan for how you want to experience them.

Give all the time you need to any change you may need to make as you go forth to collect all the nows you have remaining. And then share what you have concluded from this process:

The Unexpected Gifts Life's Turnings Can Provide

"I can finish any task I set my sights on when I take it one moment at a time." This quote from *Each Day a New Beginning* has the capacity to make our lives manageable if we take it to heart. Far too many of us focus on the project's completion, thus missing out on the joys of each step along the way. Whenever we take our sights off of this moment, this tiny step of the project, we have turned our backs on what living actually means.

I spent years of my life in never-never land. I wasn't even conscious of the actual process of living. I was just going through the motions completely inattentively. That may sound familiar to you too. But you and I have turned a corner. That corner brought us to this very spot where we are in communication with each other at this very instant through this workbook.

In this specific moment, we can look at life with actual joy and commitment to receiving every gift it is offering us. Every moment does indeed promise us a gift, one that when opened carries us to the next gift too.

I love reviewing some of the gifts I have received, virtually none of which I could ever have guessed were headed my way. Getting divorced in 1971 had not been on my radar. Nor had earning a doctorate crossed my mind. One of the biggest ones, of course, was my sobriety. I had no idea on May 24, 1976, that my life was going to head in a new direction as I walked through the doors of the St. Paul Episcopal Church in Minneapolis.

That change of direction changed everything. And here you and I meet. We may well have met in other books before now. I didn't know—I couldn't even have guessed—that God had selected me to spend my life as I have done. It has been an unimaginable gift. But no matter what God might have had in store, it would have been perfect for me. And whatever God had in store for you was perfect as well.

I think it's the right time for you to review your many gifts. Each moment offered you one. Some may not have seemed like a gift in the moment it came calling, but looking back is what provides us with a changed perspective. Why don't you look back at some of your many moments now? Which ones do you want to recount here? Take some time to contemplate first if needed. You have all the time you need.

Share here:

_____

_____

_____

_____

_____

_____

_____

_____

_____

_____

_____

Living Each Moment with Intentional Awareness

Is there really any point in having dreams and aspirations if our lives are on a predetermined trajectory of nows? Of course, the answer is yes. Those as-yet-unfulfilled dreams are the nudges we have received from the God of our understanding. And they are quite intentional and part of the bigger collection of "nows" for our lives.

This philosophy doesn't always sit well with everyone. And it wasn't a belief I embraced when I was first introduced to it either. But I have grown comfortable with it because I like the sense of security it offers me that things really won't go awry, at least not for long anyway. I may turn left or take an unplanned detour, but with God's help, I will find my way back to where I need to be. All I have to do is look at the history of my life's moments to see how this has played out.

As already said, each moment is special and always offering us exactly what we need at the time. We can ignore it. That's always our choice. But in a future moment, we will be invited once again to learn whatever we missed in the moment we ignored. Our "director" won't let us slip away forever unless, of course, that's part of the bigger plan for our lives.

But since you and I are here right now sharing this experience, we haven't slipped away. We found each other through these pages in what was assuredly a necessary moment for each of us. And what a pleasure it is to meet you here.

The best part for me of sticking to just one moment at a time is that it allows me to have a quieter mind. What's gone can't be changed anyway, so why focus on it? As the saying goes, "Even God can't change the past." I can't take back words or actions. I can make amends, but I must move on or I miss what's quite intentionally coming my way now.

I actually love the awareness that I don't need to contemplate the future at all. There is no future within sight. There is only each "now" rushing toward me, and I honestly can't miss a single one of them. Whether I take notice or not, they will come—and go. Never to return. Do I want to let them slip by unnoticed? No. Do I, far too often? Yes. But it's something only I can change. And the same is true for you too.

Are you letting the moments slip by unnoticed? What evidence do you have that this is true? What decision can you make right now to change your approach to living one moment at a time? This is worth giving some attention to before sharing. How you approach the rest of your life can change on a dime, as they say.

Meditate, contemplate, then share:

_____

_____

_____

_____

_____

_____

_____

_____

Trust in the Tides

"I will flow with the tide. It will assuredly move me closer to my destination." When I revisit this quote from *Each Day a New Beginning*, it reemphasizes the idea of staying within each moment as it comes. The tide is what it is and it comes when it should—just like the moments of our lives. The rhythm isn't ours to determine, only to live. And that makes the move forward pretty easy. Just one step at a time, one moment at a time, and we will get where we are being called to be.

Frankly, as I have aged, I have felt great relief that the future isn't mine to determine and the past is done. My mind can rest: At last. I spent many years living barely on the fringes of "now." In fact, I'd have to admit I wasn't even sure how to grasp "now." For decades, my mind was hung up mostly on the past and what "he or she" should have done. And when it came to the future, I was terrified about what might happen. *Would he leave?* Indeed, he did. Today it makes me smile. Did my anticipation create my future? Some would say yes.

I remember seeing the book *Be Here Now* by Ram Dass at my husband's home long before we married. I was intrigued by the way it was written. You had to read it in a circular fashion. It was a clever way to get across the author's point, and it definitely made being in the moment necessary. At that time, I wasn't even aware of how far in the future I usually lived. I would have resisted the idea that I could actually experience life in any other way.

Am I consistently living one moment at a time today? Of course not. Do I want to be here now? Indeed I do. I've already pretty well explained why, I think. It simply makes life less stressful. At eighty-five, I've had enough stress for any lifetime. Perhaps you feel the same, regardless of how many years you have been walking around this planet. Truth be told, there isn't any good reason for any of us to ever be stressed by an event in our lives. Each one of them is making a visit in the company of God, and we can trust that all is well.

I sure wish I had adopted this understanding when I was a younger woman. Heck, I wish I had realized this in my childhood. I spent so many years in my youth eternally anxious beyond words. To realize now that I could have walked through all of those experiences untethered to fear; I just didn't know. I didn't know. But all is different now. I hope you are free from stress in this moment. It's the only moment you have.

Take some time here and now to think about the many nows that you might have wasted tethered to fear. Way too many, no doubt. But you are free now. Free: What does this mean to you in this very moment?

Share your thoughts here:

_____

_____

_____

_____

_____

_____

_____

_____

_____

Feet Firmly Grounded in the Now

"Stay where your feet are planted." This is a commonly repeated suggestion in twelve-step rooms. And the reason is obvious. It is far too easy to revisit what has already happened and can't be changed. None of the past can be altered—nary a single aspect of it. And what may show up in the future so easily attracts our attention too. But neither of those times can offer us the peace of mind that living in this moment, where our feet are planted, can.

To stay here, in this moment, is really quite calming once we get the hang of it. It does eliminate the worries that being anyplace else might thrust on us. Let's not forget that God is present, right here and now, and we can fully trust that whatever heads our way is right on schedule.

We can choose to worry, of course. That's always an option. But what a waste of precious time. And worry prevents us from gathering all the gifts that each moment is offering us. What we need to learn next on this journey is always coming our way. Successive lessons are on the way, in fact. And we agreed to experience each one of them! So being right here, now, where our feet are planted is all we ever have to do to fulfill the will of God.

This is one of the suggestions I heard early on in AA. It didn't register at all initially. And I have to admit, even today, my mind often goes to places other than right here and now. My ego doesn't support my need to be at peace. And as I learned from my study of *A Course in Miracles*, the ego speaks first, it speaks loudest, and it's always wrong! It wants me to worry and be fearful of what might come next. It isn't the pathway to God or peace of mind.

I have discovered that I can get back on track though, but not without intention. God never closes the door. Of course, that means peace is never more than a choice away.

Do you find staying where your feet are planted a helpful suggestion? I sure hope so. It will make the difference between living a calm, serene life and being off kilter—the two choices available. Hopefully you have had some experience with *staying put,* so to speak, and perhaps doing so has taught you something. For sure it should have offered you moments of quiet, and it's in the quiet that we can better hear the voice of God.

Take some time to think about this suggestion. Have you practiced it in the past? If so, what did it offer you? Recalling what we gained by staying where our feet are planted makes staying there even more appealing in the future.

Refresh your memory, then share here:

_____

_____

_____

_____

_____

_____

_____

_____

_____

Nellie's Wisdom

This very moment is calling to you. It's the only moment you have. And it's like no other moment that has previously called to you. Each one is unique and asking something different from us. What does this idea mean to you? That's the only question you ever need consider, as a matter of fact. What does "now" want from me? Perhaps my full attention is all that's called for. How hard can that actually be?

I had no idea how to even embrace the concept of now before coming into this recovery program. And to tell you the truth, I didn't pick up on the depth of its meaning for many of my recovering years. I guess you'd have to call me a slow learner. And even today, forty-eight years sober, I slip away from being attentive just to this moment way too often. And when that happens, my mind wanders into places it need not go.

I'm not sure why it's so hard for some of us to embrace this concept. I think we were raised by parents who far too commonly lived in the past and the future, so we "came by it honestly," as the saying goes. But missing out on the only time that really matters is missing out on what it means to be alive. And what a pity that is.

I have watched my dog Nellie, a lovely yellow Labrador, to gather clues for being in the now. Dogs always are, you know. And she simply responds to what's in front of her. That's the primary clue for each of us to embrace: Take note of what's in front of you. That's all that matters. That's all there is that counts.

I'd like to suggest you spend the next few minutes simply paying attention to what is right before you. What do you see? Write it down. What do you hear? Write that down too. And what thought are you thinking at this moment? Is it about the here and now? Or is it about the past or the future? Write down where your mind is right now. We have to willingly practice staying in the present if we want to gather all that it has to offer. Are you up for the idea of refocusing your mind?

It's time to share. What comes to you as you look at the questions posed in the preceding paragraph? We need to see where we are if we want to move somewhere else.

_____

_____

_____

_____

_____

_____

_____

_____

_____

_____

_____

_____

Unwritten Chapters

The title of this chapter is "Now Is Our Time." What do you dream of doing right now that you have never dared to attempt before? None of us knows how many "nows" we have left on this planet, so if there is something that has always called out to you, right now might be the right time to give it a go.

Some say our dreams are God inspired. Who knows if that's true, but the dream came from somewhere, and since our "nows" are limited, perhaps it makes sense to pay them heed before it's too late.

I'm assuming you have contemplated how you might want to spend some of the precious "nows" you have left. I surely have. For one thing, I want to write a memoir. I want to enjoy once again the experiences that gave my life purpose and depth before my time has run out.

Admittedly, writing a memoir takes me back into the past, but I don't see that activity as dwelling on the past in an unhealthy way. I see it as paying homage in an appreciative way to those stages of my life that enriched me in myriad ways. And I also believe, quite completely, that every stage I experienced needed to be lived in order for me to be sitting here today, writing this very book that you are now holding.

As I've said many times in other chapters, nothing we lived through was for naught. I know I needed every single encounter; I needed to grow in all the ways I grew; I even needed to experience the tough times as well. They were part of my learning curve. Looking at my life from that perspective, which is one you too might want to consider using, is hopeful, I think. At least it has convinced me that every single "now" that is yet to come will be its own blessing.

How many moments remain for you—for any of us—is the big unknown; however, the time to act is *now* if there is something that calls to you. There may not be any better place to be than on the edge of something potentially exciting. And if it has called, now is surely its time. And you are surely being invited to trust the calling.

What is this idea saying to you right now? Where might it be leading you? Share your thoughts here:

_____

_____

_____

_____

_____

_____

_____

_____

_____

_____

_____

Here and Now

Eckhart Tolle says, "It is through gratitude for the present moment that the spiritual dimension of life opens up." And I'm wondering how many of you reading this right now are truly feeling grateful for this present moment.

It's not always easy to stay in the present moment. How well I know. My struggle is quite like yours, I'm sure. Our ego minds want to pull us into the past or push us into the unknown future. But right here, right now, within the embrace of God, is where all is well. This embrace is peace personified. Why would we choose to be anyplace else? Why indeed?

Yet my mind is at times inclined to wander. And I doubt that any of you reading this live comfortably, every moment, only in the here and now. It's our natural inclination to revisit the past and fret about what might happen in the future. How well I know both of these stopping off points.

But how do we stay right here in the present moment and nowhere else? Can it be done through sheer determination? Or perhaps the willingness to surrender? Or a bit of both?

I know from many years of personal experience how elusive connecting with and then embracing just this moment can be. And I know too that unless I am able to turn my will over completely to my Higher Power, I will not know peace in any sustained way. I simply have to keep doing what I know best to do, and that's to remember what I know to be true. I need not be ashamed of my forgetfulness. God doesn't mind. He's not going anyplace.

He has signed up for my journey. Whatever twists and turns my path may take, He is along for the ride. For this you and I can be constantly grateful. He will never lose sight of us—*never*.

How does it make you feel to know that God is present for every moment of your journey through life? I find it calming and reassuring. I hope you do too. I hope it heightens your gratitude to know you are now and always will be in good hands—that any time in the past when you might have felt lost, you were still within God's view. Nothing will ever change that—nothing at all.

There is a lot to absorb here. Give yourself time to dwell on this section and allow Eckhart Tolle's quote above and your awareness of God's constancy to comfort you. Then share whatever thoughts you have. You have come down the homestretch. God is waiting to hear from you whenever you are ready:

_____

_____

_____

_____

_____

_____

_____

_____

_____

_____

_____

Concluding Thoughts

We have traveled far in this workbook. And we have discovered how our stories have been influenced by all the stories we have encountered. We are not isolated, one from another—not at all. And that's due to the intention of our Creator. We have met whom we needed to meet. We have served as teachers to them and have also been taught by all those people who have crossed our path. As I have repeatedly said, there have been no accidental encounters during any part of our lifetime. And any encounter on our horizon is intentional too.

It's my hope that from the first chapter until the end of the last chapter you have been inspired to revisit the stopping off points of your life. Our lives have indeed been purposeful. Most of us might not have appreciated that fact in the midst of an experience, and that's okay. We have been here meeting our companions quite by intention. And since we are still here reading these words, it can only mean we have more encounters on the way.

Was there one chapter that spoke to you even more than the rest? If so, you might want to review it again and see if you can determine why. And was there a chapter that you hurried through because you weren't all that interested in what I was suggesting that you consider? If so, perhaps it's worth a second look. We aren't always ready for what is heading our direction. As I have said a multitude of times, postponing what's on the horizon until a later time is always a choice we have. However, we will indeed be called to address the lessons we need at some point—we can delay these steps, but they're still waiting there for us to take.

This workbook has been designed for you to make of it what you wish. You can tuck it away now if you feel done with it, perhaps to retrieve it next year to review your thoughts from this period of time. It just might be that you would answer or respond to my suggestions far differently the next time you take a look. And that's good. It likely means you are growing and are aware of your growth.

None of us will ever quit growing until that last breath is taken. Hallelujah. And this makes for a pretty exciting journey yet to come. Enjoy every moment of it. What's coming is meant for you alone.

I'd love to hear from you and encourage you to reach out to me with any comments or questions you may have. Please feel free to send these to me via email at: karencasey@me.com.

You are invited to take a look at my blog and more on my website: http://www.womens-spirituality.com.

I am on Facebook with occasional posts. Find me at: https://www.facebook.com/karen.casey.121.

Check out my Instagram here: @KarenCaseyAuthor.

Stay well and hopeful. We are here to show each other the way.

About the Author

Karen Casey, winner of a 2007 Johnson Institute America Honors Recovery Award for her contributions to the field, is a sought-after speaker at recovery and spirituality conferences throughout the country. She has written thirty-one books, among them *Each Day a Renewed Beginning: Meditations for a Peaceful Journey, Peace a Day at a Time, 52 Ways to Live the Course in Miracles, 20 Things I Know for Sure, It's Up to You, Codependence and the Power of Detachment*, and *Change Your Mind and Your Life Will Follow*—a bestselling book that is the basis for her Change Your Mind Workshops—plus many more. This workbook you hold in your hands is based upon Karen Casey's first daily meditation book, which was originally published in 1982, has sold more than four million copies, and has been translated into ten different languages.

To learn more about Karen's work, visit her on:

Instagram: @KarenCaseyAuthor
Facebook page: facebook.com/karen.casey.121
or check out her website at: www.womens-spirituality.com.

Mango Publishing, established in 2014, publishes an eclectic list of books by diverse authors—both new and established voices—on topics ranging from business, personal growth, women's empowerment, LGBTQ studies, health, and spirituality to history, popular culture, time management, decluttering, lifestyle, mental wellness, aging, and sustainable living. We were named 2019 *and* 2020's #1 fastest growing independent publisher by *Publishers Weekly*. Our success is driven by our main goal, which is to publish high-quality books that will entertain readers as well as make a positive difference in their lives.

Our readers are our most important resource; we value your input, suggestions, and ideas. We'd love to hear from you—after all, we are publishing books for you!

Please stay in touch with us and follow us at:

Facebook: Mango Publishing
Twitter: @MangoPublishing
Instagram: @MangoPublishing
LinkedIn: Mango Publishing
Pinterest: Mango Publishing
Newsletter: mangopublishinggroup.com/newsletter

Join us on Mango's journey to reinvent publishing, one book at a time.

Printed in the USA
CPSIA information can be obtained
at www.ICGtesting.com
JSHW031233060324
58611JS00005B/6